YOUNG BROKE & BEAUTIFUL

broke-ass stuart's
guide to living cheaply

Broke-Ass Stuart with **Jill Strominger**

Seven Footer Press
247 West 30th Street, 2nd Floor
New York, NY 10001

First Printing, June 2011
10 9 8 7 6 5 4 3 2 1
Copyright © 2011 by Stuart Schuffman

ISBN-13: 978-1934734-23-0

Design and illustrations by Mike Force
Cover by Michael Ebert for IFC

Introduction	5
Who the Fuck is Broke-Ass Stuart?	7
Broke-Ass Manifesto	10
Eating	11
Traveling	37
Shopping	77
Making Money	91
How to Be Broke	107
Entertainment	111
Drinking	131
Dating for Broke-Asses	151
Health	171
Beauty	181
Financial Stuff	193
Contributors	215
Thanks	220

"You look back and see how hard you worked and how poor you were, and how desperately anxious you were to succeed, and all you can remember is how happy you were" – Jack London

"You are Young, Broke and Beautiful" – Broke-Ass Stuart

Introduction

Everyone keeps saying times are tough, which is probably true–if you're a sucker. But you, my friend, are not a sucker. I can tell this simply by the fact that you're holding this book. By picking it up you're saying, "I might be broke, but, fuck it, that doesn't mean I can't have fun." And that's what I'm here to show you.

You are young, broke and beautiful–and simply by being so you're one step ahead of all those douchebags who are slaves to their salary. I'd rather be broke and happy than rich and working too much. Know what I mean?

This book isn't simply just a guide to living cheaply. It's a testament to the fact that you don't have be rich to enjoy your life. You don't have to have designer clothes and expensive things to prove that you're amazing. What makes life interesting is not the things that you own, but the shit that you do. This book is also about using the resources you already have to enrich your brokeitude. Not only does it have tips and websites to help you get through your daily grind, it's also full of the funny stories and anecdotes that come from a broke ass life well lived. If this is what you were looking for when you picked up this book, well, pal, you've come to the right place. If not, I think Rachael Ray's got a book one aisle over–sucker.

No, I'm not asking for change. I'm seeing if you wanna try on my hat. But well, if you do happen to have some spare change... photo by Julie Michelle (ILiveHereSF.com)

Who the Fuck is Broke-Ass Stuart?

I was working in a candy store in San Francisco when all this madness started. One day, an older kid from my neighborhood in San Diego, came into the store with his fiancé (they're married now). Since it had been years since I'd seen him, it was really nice to hear what was going on in his life. After we chatted for a bit, and they bought some candy (I slang candy like a motherfucker), the fiancé handed me her card and told me that I should give them a shout next time I was in San Diego. After they left, I looked at her card, and it said she was a travel writer. I thought to myself, "Travel Writer? I wanna be a travel writer," and it was then that I decided to be one.

If you know where to look, San Francisco is a town full of cheap places to eat and drink, so when it occurred to me to write *Broke-Ass Stuart's Guide to Living Cheaply in San Francisco*, I had already built up a nice array of fine establishments (meaning dive bars and greasy spoon diners) from which I could draw inspiration. I was pretty fucking broke at the time (still am), and so was everyone else I knew. I figured I would put something together to help out all other young struggling folks in the City. The original *Broke-Ass Stuart's Guide to*

Living Cheaply in San Francisco was a 33 page zine, with the only photo being the cover shot, taken in the basement of my girlfriend at the time's apartment building in the Tendernob. The first run, of only 50 copies quickly sold, so in the next run I printed 100. It was with these 100 copies that I started hitting up bookstores around the City and somehow talking them into not only carrying them, but also in some cases putting them up near the checkout counter. I sold an amazing 1,000 or so copies of this first zine and won the "Best Local Zine" in the *SF Bay Guardian*'s Best of the Bay issue. Truthfully, my reaction to this minor success was, "Holy shit! I can't believe people really dig this stuff."

By the time *Broke-Ass Stuart's Guide to Living Cheaply v.2* came out in July 2005, this shit had gotten a lot of hype, so I threw a big release party with bands, DJ's, free food and a whole bunch of other crap. Broke-Ass v.2 is when everything really took off; I sold 300 copies of it in the first week (remember this is a zine with no PR and I was doing all the distribution by foot and mass transit). Lots of good things came about because of it; I was on TV a few times, on the radio, got "Best of the Bay" again, people recognized me at bars, I had some groupies, and ultimately, I got to write for *Lonely Planet* (I did the Ireland chapter for the Western Europe and Europe on a Shoestring books). I was finally, officially, a travel writer; I even had business cards that said so.

After Ireland I decided that doing everything myself was too much work, and that if I was gonna continue to do the whole Broke-Ass Stuart thing, I wanted to have a publisher so all I would have to do is write books, and let them handle the rest. I blew every guy in Hollywood before I realized that the publishing industry was based in New York. Then (this part is actually real) I found Seven Footer on Craigslist, and conned them into putting out my books...suckers.

Broke-Ass Stuart's Guide to Living Cheaply in San Francisco came out as an actual book in November 2007, and I celebrated once again by throwing a party with bands, DJ's, free food, clowns, and even fucking laser projections. This time 700 people showed up and there was a line around the block...holy shit was that crazy. Then *Broke-Ass Stuart's Guide to Living Cheaply in New York City* came out in November 2008, and I once again celebrated with a big ass 700 person party, this time in New York. I've gotten pretty good at this whole throwing parties thing.

So here we are. I've come a loooong way (and so have you if

broke-ass manifesto
for stuart

broke as we might be, we are not breaking, we are beautiful
riding bicycles, caltrain, muni, serving PBR and well drink
specials, wearing neckties and highheels, working late nights
and over-time, taking snapshots of rooftops, pigeons,
homeless people, looking for we don't know quite what and
trying to say it we don't know how but we open our mouths
and trust the right words will pour out like some kind of
gold at the end of some kind of rainbow because we are
lovers and haters and hipsters and geeks, writing poems
in the street, spray painting buildings, making DIY and
everything indie and shabby oh so chic, hanging home-made
art in coffee shop galleries, reading books without covers
and checking out movies from the public library. we are
attracted like moths to candle flame to what is free,
what is worth bartering, what will keep our frugality and
tight wallets from emptying, all for the sake of a
happiness we're not sure we can claim, but we keep on,
dancing costumed in the street, sitting next to you
silently, shouting, we are broke, we are beautiful, and
we are not breaking.

by Silvi Alcivar
(ThePoetryStore.net)

you've actually read this entire section). What started out as a zine that I sold from my backpack is now a series of books and a popular website. Plus I even have my own goddamn TV show on IFC. Can you believe that? Me neither.

What you're now holding is *Young, Broke and Beautiful: Broke-Ass Stuart's Guide to Living Cheaply.* I poured a couple years of my life into writing and researching this book, and I'm glad that it has found its way to you. I don't want to say that it's fate, because I don't believe in that shit, but you and I have both made the decisions that have landed this book in your hands, at this particular point in history. And so for that, I just want to say, I love you motherfucker. I hope you enjoy reading this book as much as I enjoyed researching and writing it.

Broke-Ass Stuart

This is why I can't have nice things. (VictoriaSmithPhoto.com)

Eating

Your stomach shouldn't be empty just because your wallet is." Eating can be one of the most enjoyable or most annoying experiences of being alive, depending on how much that shit is costing you. Here's a little guide to help make it more of the former.

Ethnic 'Hoods

All cities have neighborhoods where immigrants gather en masse to live, eat, talk and exist in a manner similar to the land they came from. Whether it's called Chinatown, El Barrio, Le Petite Senegal, East L.A. or something else that sounds like it's full of not-white people, this is the place you want to go to find awesome cheap food. All you have to do is have an open mind about food and willingness to try new things. Also: You can't be a pussy.

Often these neighborhoods are not the nicest parts of town;

immigrants to Boston aren't gonna be moving up to Beacon Hill with John Kerry right away—you know what I mean? So beyond being willing to try new culinary delights, you have to be willing to go into parts of your city that you have yet to explore. Now, I'm not telling you to walk through East Harlem at 2 a.m. screaming, "Give me Mexican food or give me death!" I'm just saying that a lot of "bad" neighborhoods are not as bad as the media makes them out to be. Just as in any neighborhood you've never been to before, as long as you're smart about when you go (depending on the neighborhood) and how you behave (don't flash your cash or listen to your iPod), you will should be absolutely safe.*

Farmers' Markets

You probably already know this, but farmers' markets are badass. You can get fresh, and often organic, vegetables and fruits grown nearby at great prices. Plus, for those of you who aren't really into the whole fruit-and-veggie thing, you can often find stands selling everything from cheese to free-range meat to delectable samosas (like the dude in Santa Cruz, California. Fuck, those are good!). And generally speaking, a whole lot of the stands give out free samples so you can get half-full for FREE. So go feed yourself and support some farmers, dammit! This could also be a great way to meet attractive people who share your strong interests in being cheap and eating delicious things (as long as you can handle the smell of patchouli). Locate your nearest farmers market by going to localharvest.org

Bodegas

In case you haven't figured it out yet, bodegas (a.k.a. corner stores) are your best friends. They are there to sell you cheap sandwiches and hot food at any hour of the day, allow you to buy beer until 4 a.m. (or 2 a.m., depending on where you live), and provide the local neighborhood gossip. Be good to these people, and not just because they are hard-working folks who deserve your respect. Become buddy-buddy with your bodega guys because they will save your ass. They are always around; they've got constant eyes and ears on your block. I know it sounds crazy, but trust me on this one.

---

*Broke-Ass Disclaimer: Stuart is not liable for anything if you do get mugged and/or beaten up.

Get Down With the Hare Krishnas

The first vegan I ever met was my friend Sarah. She was also the first of my friends to move out of her parents' house. We were about 16 when she moved out. Since she was so young, it was hard for her to get a job that paid well, and Sarah was always superbroke. Luckily for her she lived in San Diego's Pacific Beach* neighborhood and was within walking distance of the local Hare Krishna Temple. Every Sunday they made a giant veggie/vegan dinner, and she'd go down there and eat for cheap. They always had a cheaply priced suggested donation and it was all-you-can-eat. So what's the moral of this story? Find out where your nearest Hare Krishna Temple is and attend their weekly feast. Be warned you may have to sit through some chanting, but I know you've endured far worse for a cheap meal.

Food Not Bombs

If you're hungry but ain't got no money, then Food Not Bombs is just for you. Started in Cambridge, Massachusetts, in 1980 by a bunch of anti-nukes activists, FNB now shares FREE vegan and vegetarian meals in over 1,000 cities around the world every week to protest war, poverty and the destruction of the environment. Not bad, eh? All you gotta do is show up wherever they are and your ass will get fed. Bonus: Just by eating their food you are doing important shit like protesting war and hunger. Good job, you! If you wanna learn more about them and find out where and when they feed people in your city go to foodnotbombs.net. Clicking on "all contacts" will start your journey toward the free foodness.

Free Restaurants

I know what you're thinking, and no, a free restaurant does not mean you dine and dash (a.k.a run out on the bill). There are actually a handful of restaurants scattered throughout the U.S. (and the world) that will feed anyone who shows up, and ask only that you donate what you can. There's Potager Café (PotagerCafe.com) in Arlington Texas, So All May Eat (SoAllMayEat.org) in Denver, Curry Without Worry (CurryWithoutWorry.org) in San Francisco, and Karma

---

This was probably back in 1995 when Pacific Beach was actually cool–just to clarify.

Kitchen (KarmaKitchen.org) in Berkeley, California & Washington, D.C. to name a few. You can a list of more at Wiki.GiftEconomy.org/wiki/Free_Restaurants, but the list may not be complete. Please email me if you know of more of them. FYI: The food served is usually organic, vegan and more or less environmentally friendly. It may or may not come with a side of hippies.

Costco

Find a friend with a Costco card. Go to Costco. Eat as many samples as you want. Go home satisfied. Repeat. Same thing works for Sam's Club.

Free Food at Bars

My San Francisco and New York books each have a whole appendix on where to get free food at various bars. In fact, you'd be surprised how much free food is out there. Many times the grub-a-dub-dub is only at happy hour, but sometimes you'll get lucky enough to find a place that serves the stuff at other hours too.

Since I don't know what city you're in (my powers are only so limited), I can't tell you which places around you do the deed, but you can easily find out all by yourself. By using the search part of sites like chowhound.com and yelp.com you can search for keywords like "free food happy hour" and just dive in from there. It may take a bit of time and effort to play with different word combinations, but you are bound to come up with some good free eats at some point. You can try it with Google as well–using quote marks around key phrases works wonders.

Potlucks

When it comes to entertaining at home I've always been a potluck kind of guy. And by that I mean I'm lazy. Very lazy. When I was younger, the extent of my home entertaining was, "All right, dude, you buy a 40, I buy a 40, and then we can hang at my house, smoke a blunt, and play some motherfucking *Grand Theft Auto*." Then at some point in college I started going to these regular Monday night food parties, and I had a revelation: If you tell people that you're having a "potluck," they bring all kinds of food to your house. All you have to do is supply the house and maybe a case of cheap beer. That epiphany led to me throwing plenty of "bring something to share" parties, which always netted me plenty of leftovers to graze on for at least a couple days. That was, of course, when I lived with my buddies, so along with leftovers, the house was also left with a sticky kitchen floor for a few days after each party. But our slovenly habits is not the point. The point is that by having potlucks, you will always eat well and always have leftovers. You win.

If you plan on having such parties and you really wanna get into it (like cooking and shit), check out the book *Forking Fantastic!* by Zora O'Neill and Tamara Reynolds. It's a fantastic resource for entertaining large groups of people because it is 200-plus pages and has over 50 recipes. These ladies are my kind of people: The original title of the book was *Fucking Delicious.*

Restaurant.com

This shit is genius. Whoever invented it is probably doing Scrooge McDuck dives into their piles of money while their private chef prepares a lobster dinner and their three lovers get ready for bed. Or not. I really don't know what millionaires do with their money, I just know what I'd do if I was one. I'd do some seriously superfluous shit like I just described. Anyway, considering that I'm not a millionaire, and I'm willing to bet that you aren't either, we can at least get something good out of restaurant.com while its inventor does hundred-dollar-bill backstrokes.

Here's how it works: You go on restaurant.com and enter your zip code. Then the site gives you a list of restaurants near you. After picking one you get to buy highly discounted coupons to said eatery. You can often buy a $50 coupon for only $20, or keep an eye out for promotions knocking it even lower. See? Even broke-asses like us can get a nice meal for not much work.

Daily Deal Websites

By now you've seen a million different versions of this. Groupon and Living Social are the big boys on the block, but just about every city has other smaller companies doing the same thing. Hell, I even do my own version occasionally called Broke Bucks. Regardless of which one we're talking about, they all work on similar premise: Each day they run a deal for a different business that could get you up to 90% off. It's not always eateries. Sometimes it's stores, bars, and hell, even mani-pedi places. But you already know this shit, right? If not, you probably haven't heard of the Internet yet, either.

Underground Supper Clubs

One thing I know for sure is that having no money means that when have some to spend, you wanna make sure it's worth it. Can you get a fourcourse gourmet meal at a nice restaurant for $30? Maybe if you go during Restaurant Week or use a coupon site. But how would you feel about spending $30 to get a home-cooked meal and hang out with awesome people at akick-ass supper club? You'd feel like a genius, wouldn't you? You should because it's brilliant. All over the country, underground dinner parties are happening in people's houses, garages, storefronts, basements, backyards etc. Often those cooking the meals are professional chefs who just wanna do some extra work on their days off. It's a good way for them to try out new recipes and/or make some extra scratch. And you get the benefit of eating a stellar meal for a tenth of what you would've paid at the chef's restaurant. You smell me?

So, my little rebels, I bet you're wondering how to find out about these parties. Well, too bad because the first rule about underground supper club is: Don't talk about underground supper club. And the second rule is: That's the last time I make that joke. For reals, though, the first thing you should do is Google your city and "underground supper club" to find specific parties near you and sign up for their mailing lists. You can also become a member of The Ghetto Gourmet (theghet.com), and tap into different underground dinner parties networks everywhere. Just remember, this is not Red Lobster, so if you're a messy motherfucker, you gotta bring your own bib.

Grow Your Own Food

While some of you are living in places where you actually have yards and gardens, I know a lot of you think the only thing you can grow on your block is the mold in your shower. Sure, out of all the things to grow that's probably the easiest, but seriously, that shit is gross and not edible (or is it?). But guess what? You can grow your own food in your own neighborhood.

Pretty much every city has community gardens. These are places where you can help work a plot of land to grow fruits, vegetables, herbs, spices, flowers and anything else that grows in the ground. Some people do it because they find it therapeutic, while others do it to grow some grub. To find out where there's one near you, check out the American Community Gardening Association (communitygarden.org) or simply Google the name of your town and "community garden."

For those of you don't play well with others or don't know how to share, you can always start a garden on your roof! If your roof is flat and you have access to it, you can grow any number of things on it (including pot if your neighbors can't see it). Personally, I'm no expert at growing anything but older and fatter, so if you want some specifics on how to grow a roof garden it's best if you just Google "how to grow a roof garden."

Dumpster Diving

This is for those of you who spent your last pennies on this book. Dumpster diving is the practice of going through trash cans and dumpsters, generally from commercial businesses, and taking the things that were thrown away. As the old saying goes, "One man's trash is another man's treasure." A lot of my friends who dumpster dive do it in the dumpsters behind big markets like Key Food, Safeway, and Trader Joe's. You can find a lot of eatable produce. Other good places to check out are the dumpsters for bakeries, bagel stores, and specialty food places like Gourmet Garage or Whole Foods Market. Be alert, though—some dumpsters are kept locked and some stores consider them private property. If this anti-capitalist lifestyle sounds appealing to you, check out freegan.info to learn more. In fact, the site even has links to dumpster diving tutorials for those of you who need step-by-step instructions. Just click "practice," then "urban foraging."

Restaurant Week

This is pretty much the complete opposite of dumpster diving, but sometimes your grandmother dies and suddenly you're feeling flush with some extra money. Most cities have some sort of Restaurant Week , and it generally happens a few times a year. It basically allows you to dine at some of the better spots in the city while getting a great deal on a prix-fixe meal. Sometimes these are even charity events like Dining Out for a Cure (DiningOutForACure.com), which raises money for breast cancer research. This means that you're not just foolishly spending the money that Nana saved since the Depression, you're also spending it for a good cause. Either way, it's definitely a worthy splurge if you've got some extra bread to spend.

Leftovers

This seems obvious, but if you go out to eat and don't finish your food, get it wrapped up to go. Even if you don't plan on eating it later, you can give it to a homeless or hungry person on your way home. They really appreciate that sort of thing, just make sure to cut off the part of the burger you motorboated first. Just because they're hungry doesn't mean they want your germs.

Wild Foraging

I was a shitty Boy Scout and I quit pretty early on. I think the only thing I ever got out of it was winning Austin Speed's mom's cookies in a raffle. This means that if you and I are ever trapped in some remote place, I will almost certainly be a burden on you. I am not an outdoorsman, and if you aren't either, we're fucked. In case you are, though, here are some tips you might find useful. According to freegan.info: "Wild foraging is the act of harvesting edible, wild growing plants and fungi." You can get in on this stuff by just hitting up the nearest bit of nature to where you live. Hell, you can even do it in places like New York's Central Park. What? You don't believe me? Then you should check out wildmanstevebrill.com. Now, this is a cat you'd be stoked to be trapped in nature with. He's an authority on edible and medicinal plants and mushrooms. Who cares if his website is a fine example of Web 1.0? The dude is probably too busy eating dandelions to get around to updating his site.

Food Stamps

Let me begin by telling you that food stamps are not actually stamps. Disappointing, isn't it? It's like the time I watched the show *Wife Swap* and was let down when I realized it wasn't the wife swapping I read about in my dad's *Penthouse Letters* I used to swipe as a kid. Food stamps actually come in a debit card–like form that automatically gets renewed. It's that EBT (Electronic Benefits Transfer) option on the credit card machine that you see when you pay at the supermarket.

Anyway, while you can use EBT for stuff like toiletries and household goods, you can't use it for hot prepared items. Strangely enough, though, it is accepted at some chain eateries. I'm pretty sure I've seen it at Jack in the Box before. My friend Natalie*, who shared some info on food stamps with me, told me you can also use EBT at some farmers' markets in San Francisco. You might be able to use them in your town, too! Natalie nailed it when she said:

You go to the information or organizer's booth (or van in the case of the Civic Center in SF) and they'll charge your card and you get tokens specific for that farmers market, each worth $1. The Civic Center farmers' market has some really well priced pesticide-free produce, which makes it hella worth it. It also makes me feel good using my food stamps there because it's such a direct way of the government working on this shitty economy. They give me "stimulus" money and I hand it directly to someone that grew/made something in the U.S. Yay, economic growth! Or something...

To get food stamps you have to make under a certain amount of money each month, and this amount varies in every region. You also have to apply, which means that you've got take your ass down to the Social Security office and get yourself an application. They'll want to see some pay stubs and proof of residence, among other things. This is to make sure you're not some fourthrate grifter. Man, you really have to be bad at grifting if your scam is food stamps. Anyway, that's about all I can tell you on this subject. To find out more do what I said before: go to the Social Security office. Or you can go here: socialsecurity.gov/pubs/10100.html

Soup Kitchens and Food Pantries

You probably thought this would come sooner, but it's last because it should be a last resort. Real talk: These are designed for people in seriously bad situations, so please don't hit them up simply because, well, it's easy.

Awkward morality hat off now, here are differences between the two, should you decide you are indeed that broke. Soup kitchens serve prepared meals (kinda like a broke-ass cafeteria), while food pantries give out ingredients and cooking materials (like a broke-ass grocery store, I guess). In both cases the food is free, but depending

---

Thanks to Natalie from BikeBasketPies.com for breaking some of this down for me. Here's to selling enough of those pies to get off food stamps!

on the organization you might have to smile and nod during a speech about redemption and other religiousy things before getting any grub. I'll say it again: I've put up with worse for a free meal.

A plus side to using these facilities is that they're great places to score drugs! Just kidding. To find the nearest soup kitchen or food pantry to you, visit foodpantries.org.

Awesome Recipe Websites

My friend Gabi Moskowitz runs a kick-ass website called **BrokeAss Gourmet** (brokeassgourmet.com). As you can tell by the name of it, she's on our team. The site features great recipes that are always under $20. I asked her to compile a list of ten of her favorite cheap recipe sites, which she did. The needlessly infantile and buffoonish commentary is, of course, mine.

Smitten Kitchen: Solid recipes, masterful food photos and a grip of followers on Facebook. These people are better at blogging than I am. smittenkitchen.com

Pithy and Cleaver: One of the chicks who runs this site is named Shiv. With a name like that and a site with the word "cleaver" in its title, I get the feeling she's not someone I'd want to fuck with. Apparently the recipes are equally as badass. pithyandcleaver.com

Cheap Healthy Good: I've only been called one of these words before. Can you guess which? cheaphealthygood.blogspot.com

Blue Kitchen: A cooking site only for Crips? Nope, it's full of stories and recipes and updated every Wednesday. blue-kitchen.com

Simply Recipes: Simple, huh? They obviously don't know how ill-equipped I am for pretty much anything that occurs in the world. I must be some kind of Darwinian fluke. Wait, is there a recipe for that? Sounds delicious and evolutionary. simplyrecipes.com

Cooking with Amy: This one must be popular because I've heard of it before. The first photo I saw on this site was of a smiling Asian lady so I thought she was Amy. Then I clicked on the "about" tab and a picture of a smiling Jewish lady came up and it said she was Amy. Food, Jews, and Asian chicks, and it's not even a fetish site! My computer just gasped in disbelief. cookingwithamy.blogspot.com

Steamy Kitchen: Jaden has a ridiculous number of followers on Twitter. This means that she's either a pro athlete, Ashton Kutcher or has a really popular cooking website. Regardless, she must be doing something right because those glamour shots don't look cheap. steamykitchen.com

Chocolate and Zucchini: Yet another site with great recipes and fantastic photography. I'd say that I wish the photos were as good on my site, but the truth is, considering the depraved shit we write about, blurry is probably better. Who am I kidding? We steal all our pics from the Internet anyway. chocolateandzucchini.com

How to Cook Like a Broke-Ass

By Zora O'Neill (RovingGastronome.com)

In 2001, I had an adjusted gross income of $15,912.75. This would've been tight but manageable in, say, rural Indiana. But I was living in New York City, where money leaps from your pocket and runs away screaming as soon as you walk out the front door.

And yet I think back fondly on that year. I had a good roommate, just enough freelance work and time to travel. I went to Burning Man. Sure, my bank balance bottomed out every month when I paid off my credit card bill, but I wasn't carrying any debt other than student loans.

How did I live happily on so little money, in the biggest bitch of a city in America?

Simple: I cooked.

Cooking is the ultimate tool for a life of quality broke-assery. Cadging free hot dogs at dive bars can only get you so far. If you know how to cook, a whole world of cheap fun opens up: no more greasy takeout, $8 sandwiches or generic birthday dinners in expensive restaurants.

I was lucky enough to be raised by people who cooked, and we ate like kings even though we were on food stamps half the time,. But I didn't start cooking for myself until graduate school, when I had time, motivation and housemates who would eat anything. When I ditched grad school for New York, I kept cooking, even though I didn't know anyone else here who did. I was able to lure my friends out to unfashionable Astoria, Queens, just by offering to cook them dinner.

When friends would said they couldn't possibly do what I do, I started a supper club and cooked dinner at my friends' small apartments to show them anyone could have a dinner party. Later, I started another supper club with my friend Tamara Reynolds, and that inspired our cookbook, *Forking Fantastic! Put the Party Back in Dinner Party*.

But you don't have to leap right into big parties. If you're still living on take-out and free-pizza-with-beer-purchase, just a little effort will get you well beyond ramen noodles and 29-cent pot pies.

Some tips

Ditch the steak. That shit is expensive. And if it's not—well, it should be. Cheap meat is not a good idea for all kinds of reasons, and the more you can do without it, the better. I'm not saying you should become vegetarian—just that you'll have more interesting stuff in your diet if you don't make meat the centerpiece. With lots of recipes, you can usually cut the amount of meat in half and add more vegetables, and you're better off for it.

Go ethnic. Indian, Middle Eastern, Mexican—these cuisines use inexpensive ingredients (and not a lot of meat) with surprising flavors. Plus, the local Indian or Chinese market will have beautiful fresh produce and spices for half the price at your grocery store.

Don't buy cookbooks. Go to the library or check out my podcast, Cooking in Real Time (cookinginrealtime.com). Each episode walks you through cooking a full meal. And if you're the kind of person who wants to know why, subscribe to Cook's Illustrated. It's the most boring magazine in the world, but the recipes use mostly supermarket ingredients, —and they always, always work.

Make a plan. I know: You want to be spontaneous. But if you can never find time to cook, treat it like a yoga class or an a haircut appointment and schedule it.

Treat yourself at the supermarket. I shop at thrift stores, I cut my own hair for a long time, and I don't own a car. But when I go into any kind of food store, I tell myself I can have anything I want. Food makes me happy three times a day, and it's cheaper than a new pair of boots.

Make cooking your entertainment. It doesn't have to be a just-for-foodies evening with raw-milk Camembert and a duck you shot yourself. Just invite your friends over and have them help you boil pasta and make meatballs. Or they can just bring the wine. Ain't no thing.

The more you cook, the easier it gets. Your fridge will always be stocked, and your friends will ask: "So, what're you making for dinner next week?" To get into it, try some of these recipes--they're satisfying and simple enough to make just for you, but good enough to serve to visitors.

Midnight Meat Sauce for Pasta

The original version of this recipe came from the Southwest Airlines in-flight magazine, which just goes to show you that you can find good food almost anywhere you look. I've modified the recipe over the years, and you can, too. I taught this to a friend, and she often makes it without the meat and milk—just garlic, anchovy and tomato paste. With a green salad on the side, you've got a full meal. Pasta is perhaps the easiest base on which to improvise. I've listed a few other ideas at the end of the recipe.

Serves 2

4 oz. (1/4 lb.) ground beef

1 cup milk

2 tbsp olive oil

1 large garlic clove, chopped

1 anchovy fillet, coarsely chopped (or 2 tsp anchovy paste)

2 tbsp tomato paste

8 oz spaghetti (1/2 lb)

1 tbsp butter

Whole nutmeg

1/4 to 1/2 cup grated parmesan cheese

Put pasta water on, with lots of salt.

In a small bowl, mash up ground beef with milk—break up big chunks, but don't get too obsessed with making it smooth. This will look absolutely disgusting. Let sit for 30 minutes, or until everything else is ready to go—the milk will break down the meat tissue and tenderize everything.

Chop up the garlic and the anchovy and grate the parmesan cheese. While you're waiting for the pasta water to boil, tidy up or make a salad. Once the water is boiling, throw in the pasta. Put the oil on to heat in a heavy skillet over medium-high. When the oil is hot, fry the garlic and the anchovy just until golden and aromatic. Add the tomato paste and fry briefly (the oil will probably spatter a little,). Then put in the milk and meat, and start stirring and mashing up the lumps with the edge of a wooden spoon. It will still look disgusting—all brown and pet-food-like—until the tomato paste gets all mixed in, and then only a smidge nicer. Cook until the meat is crumbly and just about all of the liquid has cooked away, stirring the whole time. Take it off the heat.

Check the pasta—it should be close to done. Drain it and save a little of the water. In the bowls you'll be eating out of, mix the hot pasta with the butter, than toss the sauce on top and mix. If it's all looking kind of dry, put in a tablespoon or so of the pasta water. Grate a little nutmeg on top and top with cheese.

Other suggested pasta toppings

1. Sauté garlic and canned clams; add a splash of white wine and a handful of chopped parsley.

2. Slow-cook onions till soft and sweet. Add garlic, then a can of plum tomatoes, mashed into chunks with your spoon. Cook down a little. Add bacon. Or, for veggie-lovers: capers, rosemary or black olives.

3. Fry onions, garlic, then mushrooms. Add tomatoes and cook down. Remove from the heat and add chunks of gorgonzola. Don't stir.

4. Greek yogurt, caramelized onions and bacon—just pile on top of cooked pasta, with a lot of grated Parmesan.

Cucumber Salad

This cool, crunchy salad is a nice counterpoint to pad thai. It also goes well with just about any Asian-style stirfry. You can use any combination of shallot and/or scallion, or even red onion, and whatever kind of chili you have around. You could also add cilantro, although I don't when I serve it with pad thai because it would be redundant.

Serves 2

2 small cucumbers, or most of a large one

1 large shallot, or the white parts of 2 scallions

1/2 jalapeño, or green or red bird's-eye chili

3–4 tbsp rice vinegar

1–2 tsp water

1–2 tsp sugar

Pinch salt

Peel the cucumbers and slice lengthwise, then into half-rounds, as thin as you have patience for. Slice the shallot in thin half-rings, or the scallions in rings. Slice the jalapeno in rings, discarding the seeds if you like. Combine all this in a bowl, then add the vinegar, water, sugar and salt and stir to combine. Let sit about 20 minutes if you have the time.

Pad Thai

This has been the most popular episode of my podcast, Cooking in Real Time. The ingredients list can be a little scary, but all the odd stuff will keep in your pantry or fridge forever. Whenever you want to make this, you just have to stop off and pick up the fresh bits: tofu, shrimp if you want it and can afford it, bean sprouts, cilantro, scallions and a lime.

The tamarind is the key. I buy frozen tamarind pulp in flat packs by Goya and other Latin-American brands. I've also found jugs of pre-sweetened pulp at Mexican groceries and a tar-like goo (water it down a little) at Thai stores. You shouldn't ever have to mess with soaking tamarind pods and pressing them through a sieve.

For 2 dinner servings, and very generous lunch leftovers

Set to soak in very hot tap water to cover:

8 oz. rice noodles

Pat dry, then chop into 1/2-inch-or-so cubes:

3-4 oz. firm tofu

Peel the shells off:

5-6 oz. small shrimp (about 16; totally optional)

Set in separate bowls:

1 or 2 shallots, diced fine and 2 garlic cloves, minced fine

2 eggs, lightly beaten with 2 tsp water and a large pinch salt

Green parts of **2 to 3 scallions**, sliced in 1/2 inch pieces (on a diagonal looks prettiest)

2 to 3 tbsp sweet preserved radish or turnip, in slivers (optional, but adds chewy sweetness)

1 to 2 tbsp tiny dried shrimp, chopped coarsely (optional, but adds a nice extra layer of shrimpiness—especially good if you're not using fresh shrimp)

For the sauce,—you may want to make extra of (it keeps in the fridge):

1/4 cup rice vinegar

1/4 cup fish sauce

Generous 1/4 cup tamarind concentrate

Scant 1/4 cup sugar (or whatever to taste)

Large pinch cayenne pepper (or whatever to taste)

Garnishes (scale back if you're saving some noodles for leftovers):

2–3 cups bean sprouts, rinsed (these can just stay in your salad spinner to drain)

1/2 cup roasted, unsalted peanuts, coarsely chopped

Green parts from **1 to 2 scallions**, sliced in 1/2-inch pieces

Leaves from **half a bunch or so of cilantro**

2 limes, quartered

When you've got everything prepped–or at least everything up to the garnishes–heat up a big cast-iron skillet (no need for a wok) on high.

Add a **big glug of peanut oil** (vegetable oil is fine too)

Then toss in the tofu and fry, without stirring, until the tofu has a little crispiness on one side; stir to flip the cubes over and fry a bit longer. (This will take longer than you think, so you can use this time to prep the rest of your garnishes.) Then remove the tofu from the pan and set back in its bowl.

Add a little more oil to the pan if it's looking dry, then toss in the shrimp and spread them out in a single layer. As soon as you see pinkness creeping up the sides, flip them. By the time you're done flipping them over, the first ones can come out. The total cooking time here is 1 minute at the absolute max. Remove and toss them in with the tofu.

Add a little more oil to the pan, then toss in the shallots and garlic. Fry until fragrant and just brown.

Then add the eggs, and stir a little and fry until set. Break into chunks with your spoon.

Drain the noodles, if you haven't already, add them to the pan and give them a quick stir. Pour in the tamarind sauce mixture. There will be a lot of liquid. Turn the heat down to medium and let the noodles simmer for about 1 minute, just until the noodles have absorbed a lot, but not all, of the liquid—there should still be visible sauce in the bottom of the pan.

Toss in the scallions and the preserved radish. Fry just until the scallions wilt (you might want to crank up the heat again very briefly). Finally, after about another 30 seconds, when the noodles are sticky but not dripping in sauce, turn off the heat, but leave the pan on the burner as you stir in the shrimp and tofu. (If in doubt, turn off the heat early—you don't want your noodles to dry out and glom together.)

Let everything sit in the pan for a minute to let the flavors meld. Serve on plates, topped with bean sprouts, cilantro, peanuts and squeezes of fresh lime.

Green Salad

My parents taught me, and I'm going to teach you: Eat a green salad every day. It drove me insane that we always had to eat one—even with vegetable soup (which already has vegetables... duh!), but there is something great about adding a little raw crunch to an otherwise all-cooked meal.

All you've got to do is wash some **greens** (anything but iceberg lettuce) and dry them well. If the greens have good flavor on their own—watercress, for instance, or arugula—you don't need much but dressing. But if you've got red-leaf or romaine lettuce, you'll want some other stuff—carrots, shreds of red cabbage, whisper-thin slices of red onion, toasted almonds, grated Parmesan, that kind of thing.

Then you make your **salad dressing**. The French call it a vinaigrette, but they also recommend a 3:1 ratio of olive oil to vinegar, which I find way too oily. So start light on the oil, but adjust everything to your own taste. Skip the fussy whisk or blender–just shake everything up in a jar with a tight-fitting lid. You can stash it in the fridge if you have any left over..

  1 clove garlic

  Dab of Dijon mustard

  Red wine vinegar

  Olive oil (the good kind)

  Salt and pepper

Squeeze the garlic through a garlic press, or chop very fine, and place in jar. Add a dab of mustard about the same size as the garlic. Add red wine vinegar, about a knuckle deep. Pour in just a bit more than twice as much olive oil. Add salt and pepper, screw the lid on the jar and shake. Taste by dipping a leaf of lettuce in. If you're finding it's too tart but don't want to add more oil, a drizzle of water can smooth the sharp edges. Or add a pinch of sugar or drizzle of honey. You can of course also vary the kind of vinegar, add shallots instead of garlic, add yogurt for creaminess and plenty more. Feel free to experiment.

Broke-Ass Porn

Once a week at brokeassstuart.com we present Broke-Ass Porn. It's visually stimulating material for the financially impaired. If this shit doesn't get you going, you're not as broke as you thought:

Leftovers

It's the day after Christmas. You are swollen, gassy, and already stretching out your sweatpants. But no: the eating still won't stop. There's still half of grandma's pie left, not to mention all the ham, turkey, bread rolls, and whatever else it is that you non-Jewish people eat on Baby Jesus' Birthday. Maybe lasagna? All I know is that there are tons of it leftover and by the time you read

this you'll already be thinking about heating some of it up.

I've always said that leftovers are my favorite meal. It's like, "Hey remember that awesome thing that I ate last night? Wouldn't it be sweet if I could have it for breakfast? Oh wait, here it is!" And the gorging cycle starts all over again. The people who own gyms are probably looking at catalogs as we speak, trying to figure out what to buy with the guilt money you're gonna spend on January 2nd. I know I'm already looking in the mirror and thinking. "Stuart, you twisted bastard. Did you really need to eat the *entire* pumpkin pie at the Alibi's FREE food spread last night? Couldn't you have at least saved some of it for that lady with no teeth? It might have been the only thing she would've been able to slurp down (not the crust of course)." Well, we all know the answer to that one, don't we?

So here's to leftovers and saying "Fuck it! I'm gonna start going to the gym again after New Year's." I figure I've got at least a week more of bingeing before it starts being considered excessive again.

How to Behave in a Restaurant

You know how in places like Israel and Switzerland it's mandatory for every citizen to spend a certain amount of time in the military? I've always thought that it should be the same in the U.S., but that instead of the army or navy, Americans should have to be in the food-service industry for six months. I honestly believe it would make us a hell of a lot nicer and more considerate to each other.

Many of us broke-asses have toiled as restaurant employees at some point or another because it's a way to have a flexible schedule while still making decent money. For those of you this applies to, I'm dedicating this piece to you. For those of you who've never worked in a restaurant, please pay attention to the following so you don't make an ass out of yourself:

Be respectful. Do not, by any means, snap your fingers at your server or call out "Waiter!" Who the hell do you think you are, Frank Sinatra? Servers are people, not fucking puppies. If you need something, make eye contact with them and smile. Chances are you were next on their list of people to get to, anyway. What people probably don't realize is that waiting tables is like playing chess, good servers are always thinking 10 steps ahead of whatever task they are currently doing.

Similarly, don't interrupt a server while they are talking with another customer. The world does not revolve around the fact that you need an extra side of salad dressing. Your business is very much appreciated....just as much as the person who's in the middle of being helped. Simply wait until the server is done with the current customer and then say, "Excuse me..." and follow with your request.

Also, this should really go without saying, but be polite. Saying "please" and "thank you" should really be part of your normal conversation skills at this point in your life.

Mind your children. I love kids. They are cute little creatures that move around and act like people. But no matter how precious your child might be outside of a restaurant, they are little fireworks of liability once inside. Think about it: If a client came into your office, made loud screeching noises when they didn't get what they wanted, winged spoons and Cheerios across the room, and then left a giant mess when they departed, they would be called "assholes" and you would stop doing business with them. Right? Now why do you think it's O.K. to let your children do that in a restaurant?

Look, I realize that raising kids is not easy, especially when they are just figuring out how awesome it is to have motor skills. But your job as the adult is to clean up after your progeny. I'll make it easy for you: Google "Kiddopotamus Tinydiner Placemat," buy one, and then bring it with you when you dine out. Not only does it have a trough to catch everything your kid drops, but it's easy to clean and reusable. If you decide to ignore this advice and do leave big mess and tip poorly on top of it, then just be aware that karma law predicts your kids will probably grow up to hate you and there will be absolutely nothing you can do about it. So just do what's right, OK?

Don't be a squatter. Blah blah European restaurants are sooo amazing because you can sit as long as you want, and blah blah Americans should be that way too, and blah blah... Yes, that would definitely be nice, but they aren't and this is where you live, so deal with it. If a restaurant is really busy—as in there is a line of people waiting to be seated—please don't just sit there reliving the details of your eggs Benedict after you eat. It's one thing to chill for a couple minutes after your meal and finish your drink, but hanging out for longer than 15 minutes is loitering. You were once that person in line who is now waiting for you to leave, and now it's their turn to feed their hangover with fat and eggs. You're also not only holding up other patrons, but also fucking with the server's money. The fewer tables a server gets, the fewer tips they get. Servers tip out everyone else, and therefore everyone is getting less money. So do the right thing and go home to belly-rub.

Tip your server well. I get that this book is about being broke, but I can't stress how important it is to leave a good tip. Servers and bartenders are usually broke-asses just like you, and unfortunately in a position where their income is largely based upon how much cash you have in your wallet. *Travel + Leisure* magazine says that the average wage for servers in the U.S. is $4.81–like, less than how much an average beer costs in any major city. The rest of what they make is up to you. Having been a server for most of my adult life, I can't tell you how insulting it is when you bust your ass to please someone only to receive a crappy tip for no reason. Therefore I will give you a rough guide to tipping: Tip your server 20%. That number is 10% of your total bill, times two. 18% at the very least if you're strapped. If you're in a bar, tip a buck a drink.

Consider yourself a patron of the arts. Most of the servers and bartenders I know do it because it gives them enough freedom to pursue what they really want to do in life. This means that when you leave a good tip, you're helping artists, writers, actors and others survive. How's this: If you think tipping 20% is too expensive, then just get your food to go and leave a couple bucks. Tipping on to-go orders often helps supplement the income of the other restaurant employees, like hosts and busboys. Also, if someone gives you something for free, remember to tip extra. Chances are you won't get it again if you don't.

If you don't have enough money to be able to leave a tip, respect these people's livelihoods and just cook and drink at home until you do.

Alrighty, folks—now that you know how to behave in a restaurant, go out and get yourself a bite to eat. Help keep this economy afloat, dammit!

Kiley Edgely, who writes for my website and has been a server on and off for 10 years, has a few key pointers for you too:

Leave me out of it. There are customers who get mad when I set the bill slightly closer to their friend, and then their friend snatches up the bill. Or customer no. 1 will grab the bill out of my hand, leaving customer no. 2 to tell me that it was their turn to pay and that customer no. 1 paid last time. Here's the thing: I don't care who pays the bill. It's none of my business. I just care that someone pays the bill (and tips me), so I don't have to chase you down the street. To avoid this, I just throw the check onto the table and run away. If you're dining out with a friend who always pays, ask me for the check when your friend is in the bathroom. I'll be more than happy to let you take care of the bill then. Just don't suck me into your drama.

Read the Menu. This seems obvious, but so many people don't even crack it open. Instead, they ask for my "personal recommendation," as if I knew some secret entree that wasn't listed. Your server will have no problem helping you decide between two options, or elaborating on the description of an item, but taste and food preferences are incredibly subjective and your server's palate could be violently different from yours. For example: I don't eat meat and I hate strawberries. Anything I'd personally recommend is going to be from a very limited spectrum of the menu. Also, you should read the menu so you avoid ordering a peanut butter–banana milkshake in a restaurant that doesn't even have milkshakes.

Be ready when you say you are. If you're still thinking when I ask if you're ready to order, tell me that you need a few more minutes. Because in all honestly, when you make me listen to your inner monologue about ordering blueberry or chocolate chip pancakes, I'm thinking about the tables I could be bussing, coffee I could be refilling, etc. I try my best to give each table the time and attention they deserve, even when I'm crazy busy. I have a lot of tasks and customers to balance, and watching you waffle between a burger and a pork sandwich is not a good use of either of our time.

Don't leave gross garbage on the table: I'm totally cool with cleaning up your dishes, crumbs, napkins, spills, etc. But I don't need to touch your snot-ridden tissues or pry your chewed gum off of a soda glass. Restaurants have bathrooms with garbage cans. Please use them.

Broke-Ass Porn

Street Food

Much like running into an old friend on the street, food carts have a way of brightening your day. You can tell a lot about a culture by the state of its street food: what is considered holy, what is considered clean, what is considered worth waiting for, and what is considered taboo. And for us, the  broke-ass masses, there is rarely an opportunity to eat so well for so little as when we cross paths with one of these wheeled distributors of deliciousness.

From California's taco trucks to New York's dirty-water hot dog carts, the base has been built with regards to what it means to sell food from a cart. But these venerable victuals are simply a foundation for a movement toward something beautiful, experimental, and new. Today on the streets of New York, your options, from barbecue to bulgogi, your your street-food options are boundless. And in San Francisco, where the street venders are tethered by strict health codes, a sort of quiet revolution is taking place, redefining what can be considered street food.

Yes, the future looks bright for food carts, but don't think the forces of evil aren't doing their best to thwart it. In recent years crackdowns have been made on the bacon-wrapped hotdog carts in both Los Angeles and San Francisco, and street vendors in New York have dealt with similar harassment. But luckily for you and I, dear reader, there are those who believe in the inherent goodness of street food and are making it their duty to keep us updated with news of this struggle. If you're in New York, The Street Vendor Project (streetvendor.org) is your best resource; they sponsor the Vendy Awards each year for the best street food vender.

As for me, I'm just looking forward to the next time I run into San Francisco's Tamale Lady. I'm getting hungry just thinking about it.

Broke-Ass Porn

Once a week at brokeassstuart.com we present Broke-Ass Porn. It's visually stimulating material for the financially impaired. If this shit doesn't get you going, you're not as broke as you thought:

Cheap Car Rentals

It's 9:18 a.m. and I'm sitting in a motel room in Santa Barbara as I write this. I'm beginning to realize that I'm no longer running my website, it's running me. At this point "vacation" means that, instead of spending all day doing stuff for the site, I'm only fucking with it in the morning while my lady is still asleep or sunning herself by the pool like she is today.

We both decided to make this a four-day weekend and do something we've been meaning to do since we first met: take a leisurely drive from San Francisco down to Los Angeles along Highway 1. Since neither of us have a car we had to get a rental, and we wanted to do it for as cheap as possible–duh.

Luckily Becky from Keeping Your Balance (keepingyourbalance.net) informed me that we wouldn't have to pay for rental car insurance because most major banks cover it for you if you pay with a credit card! Holy shit! Talk about saving like 60 bucks! Next, we went to Hotwire.com and reserved a car for four days. Guess how much it cost us? Only $70! Dude, that's only $17.50 a day, split between two people.

So the lesson for today is that you should check with your bank to see if they cover the car insurance, and you should always reserve a car through a travel website.

Now I'm off to L.A. L.A.ter , fuckers.

Thanks Xzibit for pimping my ride!

Traveling

Travel may seem like an unlikely priority for the broke-ass lifestyle, but there are ways for *even us* to see the world, beyond visiting grandparents for Passover or going to a convention in Las Vegas (yes, I'm talking about that time you went to the AVN Expo). It won't be glamorous. You will probably have to rewear socks and eat meals consisting only of peanuts. But you will still have the incredible experiences that come along with exploration, and you'll almost certainly have a more interesting time than anyone holed up in a five-star hotel will. So start putting your liquids in a bag and read on.

General Tips for Traveling Overseas

First up: Again, I know this whole little section might seem a bit ridiculous—I mean, for fuck's sake, you're probably thinking, *Bitch, I don't have any money! How the hell am I gonna travel?* –I know. But

I advise you to take whatever money you do get at some point and hit the road for a while. I've done this almost every chance I've had and, hell, I even lived out of a bag for two years, and I promise you it's something you will never regret. Your experience will be so much more valuable than the shitty beers you would have spent the money on otherwise. In fact, being broke in another country is far better than being broke wherever you are now.

Here's the plan: Save up $2,000. Spend half on a round trip ticket to any developing country in the world. Live off the other half—which will last for months (depending on where you go). If you put all your shit in storage and give up your apartment, you'll have virtually no bills at home. Snag one of the overseas work opportunities on page 95 to and you'll be able to stay even longer. Dammit, writing this while sitting in my apartment in my underwear makes me wish I was actually taking my own advice right now. So do it for me!

Travel During the Off Season: When I went to Ireland to do work for Lonely Planet, I was there for all of January and February. Do you know how wet it is in Ireland at that time of year? Wetter than your mom after a bottle of wine and a Brad Pitt movie. But because of that there also weren't many tourists around, making everything a hell of a lot cheaper than it would be normally, including the plane tickets. That was excellent. The downside was that bus service to some of the more remote places was discontinued for the winter (and in some places, seasonal activities like vineyard visits were not available). This meant that after I had hitchhiked into a tiny town in West Cork and unknowingly deflowered a hot 18-year-old barmaid (she didn't tell me it was her first time until afterward), I had to stand in the rain and hitchhike *out* of town with the very serious fear that any passing car carried a bunch of her brothers and certainly the end of my life.

Truthfully, I don't even know if she had any brothers, or if she did why she would tell them, but regardless, I got so spooked that I paid a cabby 70 Euro to take me to the next big town. I guess what I'm trying to say is that traveling during the off season is FUCKING AWESOME!

Travel Insurance: If you are going on a trip outside of the country, I highly recommend that you get travel insurance. While it does suck to have to cough up another $100-plus after spending lots of money on a ticket, you'll appreciate it when you're on your trip and realize that in addition to losing your inhibitions the night before, you also lost your camera. Hey, at least you got the clap as a souvenir. Luckily your travel insurance will probably cover the penicillin used to get rid of that, too. For information about what travel insurer will work best for you, check out travelinsurancereview.net

Travel Light: I try to travel as light as possible and only take a carry-on whenever I can. It's easier than you think. On a trip a while back I lived out of a carry-on for two weeks. During that time I went to a wedding, filmed a TV pilot and threw a huge party in NYC—all thanks to the power of rolling up my clothes. I also take last-leg clothes (or thermal shirts from the $1 store) for layering that I won't feel bad about donating if I need more space in my bag along the way. I realize not everyone can do that, so if you do decide to check some baggage, make sure you pack only clothes in that particular suitcase. Seriously, I can't emphasize this enough: Put anything that you consider important in your carry-on luggage. Medicine, toiletries, sunglasses, camera equipment, and even your security blankie should all be in your carry-on. Luggage gets lost or stolen more often than you think, and it's easier to deal with replacing your clothes than your antipsychotic medication. For more ideas, check out travelite.org.

Make Copies of Important Documents: Most importantly your passport, but you should also copy your travel insurance documents, credit cards, and driver's license. Once you've done that, keep them separate from all the originals. If you keep your passport in your money belt (or socks! They totally make socks with little pockets in them now) all the time, keep the copy in your luggage. I've even given copies to trusted family or friends back home, or scanned them and kept them in my email in some freak case that *everything I have* gets stolen. I know it sounds crazy and even a little OCD, but it will be *much* easier to deal with the embassy in an emergency if you've got a copies of all your important info.

Secure Your Shit: Let's face it: There are some thieving motherfuckers out there who want your shit. Since they can't tell that your bag is full of dirty underwear and just leave it alone, bring a lock to secure your gear in a locker where you stay. Also lock your zipper while you're in transit. Crooks look for easy targets, so if your bag looks even slightly hard, they're better off finding an easier mark. If you get a lock that requires a combination, do yourself a favor and make sure it's one you will remember–no matter how wasted you get. I almost took some bolt cutters to my lock one time in Ireland, but luckily I was wise enough to sleep off my Guinness and try to open the fucker again in the morning, at which time I got it on the first try. If your lock requires a key to open it, make sure to keep a spare somewhere safe that's *not* inside the bag. A good place would be on a string around your neck or the fifth pocket of your jeans. Trust me on this one.

Not all places you'll stay will have lockers or other safe places to store your goods. So I'm going to make a suggestion, and it's not gonna be cheap. If you plan on doing a lot of traveling, I'd recommend getting a Pacsafe. It's basically a metal mesh sack that you put your bag in. It has a locking cord that you loop around something like a bedpost. The mesh sack makes it so people can't really slash your bag and get stuff out, and the looping it around a bedpost makes it so no one can walk away with it. I've stayed in some strange and dodgy places, and having one of these has certainly set my mind at ease. They cost around $70, but that's a lot cheaper than having to replace your belongings. You can pick one up at travel or sporting goods stores or order them online at pacsafe.com.I've also heardthat you can just getsome chicken wire and line the *inside* of your bag with itso that no one can slash through your luggage. I haven't tried this myself, but it would obviously be a hell of a lot cheaper than the Pacsafe. You might want to get an old sheet to use as a buffer between your bag and the wire so that it doesn't rip up your bag.

Public Computers: If you're using any kind of public computer (at Internet cafes, your hostel, etc.) to check your bank balance, rub it in on Facebook that you're somewhere awesome, tweet about making a sandwich, and so on, make sure to clear the browser history and the cookies when you're done with the computer. That way no one can use the info you logged in with to get access to your accounts

Plastic Bags: This might just be one of my own idiosyncrasies, but I always pack a few extra plastic grocery and resealable bags in my luggage. They always come in handy. If you have products like lotions that you fear might open or explode during travel, you can put them in a plastic bag. I also pack shoes in a plastic bag to avoid getting germs and dirt all over my clothes.

Money Conversion: If you're like me and are kinda math-retarded, doing mental calculations to figure out how much loot you're spending in another country can be downright time-consuming and, well, wrong. Go to oanda.com and print up a cheat sheet with all the currency conversions. That way, when that prostitute in Krakow charges you 300 zloty for a handy, you'll know that it's costing you $102 in good old American greenbacks.

Bring a Bandana: I am to bandanas as Ford Prefect (from *Hitchhiker's Guide to the Galaxy*) is to towels. This is, once again, just one of my weird little travel habits (we all have them), but I always bring a bandana when I travel. They can be used for just about anything. Among other things, I've used mine as: an eye mask (for sleeping in bright places), a neckerchief (for really cold weather), a head covering (for hiking in hot places), and an extra wrapping for an iPod, camera, or other breakable things. Just make sure to find out if certain colored bandanas have any special significance in the place where you're traveling. If your rag is the wrong shade in a place like South Central Los Angeles you might find yet another use for it—a tourniquet.

Towels: While the name Ford Prefect is in the air I might as well mention towels. I personally travel with a little shammy instead of a big cloth towel. Towels not only take up a lot of room in your pack, they also need a lot of time to dry. If you pack them up while still moist they get mildewy real quick. So get a shammy—hell, you can even go the ShamWow route and get more shammies than you ever thought you needed for only like $20. Just don't beat up any hookers like the ShamWow guy did. Actually, I think she ended up whooping his ass.

Pack an Extra Sheet: I've slept in some really funky places and having that extra sheet to put between me and whatever strange surface I was laying on allowed me to doze off without worrying about getting one of those weird diseases that your characters died from when you played *Oregon Trail.*

Pack One Nice Thing: When you're in France and the hot Parisian you met at a café wants to take you out dancing, you'll have something to wear. Your best bet is something black—it's universally cool, goes with just about everything, and your new date won't be able to tell if you get nervous and dribble wine down your shirt. The whole "universal cool" thing is important to keep in mind if you want to blend in instead of being the obvious tourist we've all seen wearing Big Dog T-shirts and tube socks, especially if you want to have any hope whatsoever of getting laid.

Flash Drive: This is actually more important than it sounds. See, since flash drives are so tiny, they can be easily concealed. Cameras on the other hand, not so much. So take a flash drive with you when you travel and every few days or so, put all the photos from your camera on it. You can do this at pretty much any internet café. That way if you camera gets jacked you still have the most important part: your photos! If your flash card gets full, you can always ship it home fairly cheaply and it will be waiting for you when you get back.

Power Strip: If you're gonna be traveling with multiple electronics (camera, phone, laptop, iPod, etc) it's wise to bring a power strip. You'll only have to worry about having one adapter, and you can charge all your gear at the same time.

Other Advice: To get more advice from other seasoned travelers, be sure to check out Lonely Planet's forum. It's called Thorn Tree and just about any question you have can be answered there.

Oh Yeah, One Last Thing: Don't ever become a drug mule, ever.

Cheap Airfare

Unless you're being deported, airfare can be really expensive. If you're in Europe and you're reading this, then you're probably laughing out loud and masturbating with all your ticket stubs from Ryanair or easyJet. Unfortunately those of you in the U.S. can't buy plane tickets for, like, 5 Euros, but if you shop for your tickets properly (that is, follow what the fuck I say) you can end up saving a lot of money. Here are some tips for your ass, and while they may not always be options, you will hopefully be able to benefit from these ideas at some point in your life:

Fly During Off-Peak Hours: Friday, Sunday and Monday flights are generally more expensive because that's when everyone needs to fly. It's simple supply and demand. So if you can fly on any other day of the week, you're gonna get cheaper flights. Same goes for flying at ugly times. No one wants to get up at 4am for a flight, but if you're willing to do it, you will certainly pay less than if you flew at reasonable hour. Kayak.com is a great site for comparing prices of flights at different days and times.

Be Flexible: I know that most of the time you fly, you've gotta be some place at a certain time—like your nephew's bar mitzvah or your ex's gender reassignment celebration. But if you have a job, I'm sure that you also get some vacation days. If you can be flexible and wanna do some traveling, I suggest again using Kayak Buzz (kayak.com/buzz). You plug in your nearest airport, the month you want to leave, and the region you want to visit, and it brings up the cheapest flights available. I just plugged in my info and found a roundtrip flight from San Francisco to Madrid for $590! Fuck, now I'm just teasing myself. If I had the time and money I'd so buy that ticket right now.

Another similar site is AirfareWatchDog.com. Basically, you just put in your nearest airport and it brings up a list of all the cheap flights departing from there. You can specify whether it's international, domestic, weekends and more. I just found round trip from San Francisco to Sydney, Australia for $938!!

Some other websites where you can find cheap tickets are: expedia.com, orbitz.com, travelocity.com, sidestep.com, priceline.com, vayama.com, cheapoair.com and more. I'm sure you already know all about them. What you might not know, though, is that it's best to compare the rates from as many of them as possible. They don't always have the same prices.

Spirit Airlines: If you've done some traveling in Europe, you know that they have crazy-cheap airlines on which you can get flights for like 5 Euros plus taxes. In the States we're not as lucky, unless. of course. you live in a city that Spirit Airlines flies to. If you do, Spirit might become your new best friend. Go to spirit.com and sign up for their email list and they will send you deals every week. You can get flights to beautiful places like Peru, Costa Rica, Jamaica, the Virgin Islands, Puerto Rico and Detroit, for like, $50 roundtrip (including taxes). Can I get an amen?

Get a Free Ticket: Freelance writer Kate Kotler (KateKotler.com), who used to do the DIY section of my site, has a great tip for getting a FREE plane ticket:

> If you are about to board a flight and the airline asks for volunteers to give up their seat, volunteer. Seriously. If you are not in an absolute dead rush to get where you're going, give up your seat and collect the freebie ticket. Those babies are good for a year after they are issued and usually you can fly with very few restrictions. Depending on where you were going and when the next flight is, if you end up having to travel the next day, the airline will also give you a hotel voucher. Really. Free ticket = $300 to $1,000 (depending on where you were going). Currently freebie tickets are not good for international travel, but for travel in the U.S.? Priceless.
>
> This got me to thinking, if you don't have shit to do, why not just book a ticket on a flight that you know is gonna be packed, and then go to the airport and be the first to volunteer your seat? I mean, I doubt you could do it everyday, but I bet you could do it a few times and score some free tix. Worst comes to worst, you'll just have to go wherever it is that you book a ticket for. So I guess make sure it's a place you actually want to go, like Austin during South by Southwest, and not Detroit in the winter.

Try to Plan Way in Advance: I know it sounds like common sense, but it will totally save you lots of loot on a plane ticket. If possible, buy your tickets at least 14 days ahead of time (also known as two weeks, for those of you who aren't too good with the maths).

Skip the Booking Fees: If you wanna shave a few bucks off your ticket, use one of the cheap-ticket websites mentioned above to figure out exactly what flight you wanna take and with which airline. Once you've got it all figured out, book your flight directly with the airline's website. That way you won't have to pay any of the fees from the online travel agencies. While it may not save you a heap of money, it will probably buy you a couple of rounds at the bar in whatever city you're heading to.

Improving Your Flying Experience

Unfortunately ticket prices aren't the only way they try to gouge you at the airport, so it's always good to prepare yourself before your trip. Buy your magazines and books before you leave your neighborhood. Hell, just borrow them from a friend. Also, bring your own food so you aren't tempted to buy those delicious $8 Krispy Kreme doughnuts (honestly, why are they so good?). You can also avoid buying water by bringing your own *empty* reusable water bottle, and filling it up at the drinking fountain once you pass through security.

Let's face it, we all like going places but the actual act of getting from point A to point B can be fucking lame and uncomfortable. Luckily, Andrew Dalton of dolfapedia.org, and one-time editor/writer at brokeassstuart.com,, has a few solid tips for making your flight a more enjoyable experience:

Bring your booze: I know what you're thinking – you haven't been able to bring liquids through security since forever. But let's look back at the rules: Nothing more than 3 oz. in that little carryon Ziploc. Luckily for you, the mini bottles that you usually sneak in to movies are only 2 oz. I like to pick up 3 minis of Bombay Sapphire for a reasonable $2.50 apiece because the blue bottles look like fancy hotel shampoos. Put them in with your face wash and mini toothpaste (free sample from the dentist, of course) and don't make a big scene about it when you stroll through security. Just order your favorite mixer from the free beverage service. The good thing about gin is if you're on a nefarious airline that charges $2 for soda (I'm looking at you, Allegiant), you can just ask for a cup of ice and make a very dry airplane martini.

Choose your seat wisely: Assuming you didn't wait to the last minute and you're a normal human being who purchases airfare online, you will probably have the option to choose your seats. And if you're like me, you probably can't ever decide between window or aisle. The 9-year-old in me always wants to be able to look out the window even on a cross-country redeye that I've flown half a dozen times and never once had a nice view of D.C. The occasionally insightful adult in me wants to sit in the aisle in case I put down too many $8 large beers in the airport bar. Once I overcome that personal battle, I use this handy strategy to get the most out of my choice: If you're going for a window seat, pick a row where someone has already taken the aisle seat. If you want an aisle seat, pick a row where someone has taken the window seat. People flying alone will probably use the same strategy and won't pick a middle seat unless they're desperate and the flight is totally full. If you're lucky, the middle seat will be empty and you can stow your crap there and save precious legroom. We call this Broke-Ass First Class.

Your laptop is your friend: It's no secret that the most of our domestic airlines are bankrupt, so many of the major advancements in in-flight entertainment technology haven't quite made it to those aging fleets. Even Virgin America, the zenith of Broke-Ass travel, will charge you more than your Netflix monthly fee to watch a movie. But there's still a plethora of options (legal or otherwise) you can use to save movies and TV shows to your hard drive to bring along with you. Make sure you're charged up and turn off the WiFi if there's no in-flight Internet to get the most out of your aging battery. This also comes in handy when visiting grandparents who don't have cable.

Earth Bound Travel

Despite how cheap airfare has gotten, it can still be pretty expensive. That's why god invented trains, bikes, buses and cars. I just have trouble remembering on which day he actually did it. Was it the third or the fourth?

Green Tortoise: Since I'm still sitting here fantasizing about traveling for fun and procrastinating getting into the less-exciting things like traveling by Greyhound, I thought I'd tell you about Green Tortoise. GT does these awesome trips where they load you up in a bus that can sleep up to 36 people, and they roll you places all over North and Central America. GT tours are probably the cheapest ways to see a ton, meet great new people and go a bunch of different places. But you must be down to rough it a little bit (many of their trips include camping) and not be completely adverse to chilling with hippies (the crowd can be a little granola). Yes, they do a trip to Burning Man. Check them out at greentortoise.com.

Bicycling

I vaguely recall some elementary school yard joke where a kid confuses the meanings of "having sex" and "bike riding" but I don't remember it now. I don't even know why I brought it up. I guess it's just because that's what popped in my head when I sat down to write about riding a bike. Yes, that's right, when I think of riding a bike I think about 8-year-olds telling dirty jokes. Don't you? No? Wow, this is getting more awkward by the second.

Bicycling, yes, that's what this is about. Riding a bike is an incredible way to save money. It gets you where you need to go while giving you exercise. Tell your car and gym membership they can go fuck each other. Right? Another great thing about bikes is that, since you probably can't afford a fancy one, you can often get them for pretty cheap. Thrift stores and garage sales are great places to pick them up if you're simply looking for some shit with two wheels and a chain. If you want something fancier you can always find a good used bike at a decent price on craigslist.

Just don't be a fucking moron about it. I see people riding around on their fixed gear bikes at night, wearing all black with no lights, no helmet, and *no brakes!* That is seriously some of the stupidest shit I've ever seen in my life—like on a Darwinian level. These people have the life expectancy of a cheap umbrella. If you're dumb enough to do this it's probably a good thing that your DNA will be taken out of the gene pool. Look, if you're worried about looking cool while riding a bike, you're riding it for the wrong reasons.

Now I'm not saying that you need to dress in an orange-and-yellow reflective suit like some 50-year-old orthodontist who rides to work every day, but I am saying you should mind yourself. Drivers have a hard enough time seeing cyclists in the daytime, and at night it's virtually impossible. You can get yourself both a front light and one of those backside blinking red lights for, like, $15. And you gotta protect your dome! I've seen head injury in person, and *maaaaaaan,* that shit is fucked up. You can get a perfectly suitable helmet for $30 to $40. If you can't afford to buy these things, borrow the money or put it on your credit card or, fuck, ask your mom to buy it for you. Chances are she will if she can afford to.

As for riding a fixie, if you don't want the help of gears to get you up hills, whatever, that's your thing. More power to you. But, seriously, if you're too cool to have *brakes* on your bike, you don't deserve to procreate. Do the world a favor and get a vasectomy or your tubes tied. We already have enough stupid people on this planet.

Whew…now that my tirade is done, let me just say that if you haven't ridden a bike since junior jigh, the idea of doing it again might be a little daunting. If that's the case, it's totally understandable. I recommend checking out bicyclesafe.com to see how to safely navigate on two wheels. Also check in with your city's bike coalition to see if they've got any reading material about biking in your particular city.

Bus Travel

Ugh. Even thinking about getting on a bus completely kills my travel boner. What a shitty, shitty, shitty way to travel. I mean it's O.K. for short distances, but anything over four hours and you completely understand why that dude beheaded his seatmate on a Greyhound in Canada.

What I didn't realize until I went to Argentina is that, in a lot of other places in the world, bus travel is actually pretty nice. I mean, don't get me wrong, you're still on a bus for a stupid amount of time, but a lot of the buses I've been on in Latin America even have seats that fully recline. It's like lying in a very small bed while traveling on a bus. Why am I telling you this? Mostly just to rub it in your face, but also because it's a good segue into mentioning that there are more bus travel options than just the vile Greyhound.

Chinatown Buses: Yes, the famous Chinatown Buses. These fuckers are the cheapest way to get from one city to another on the East Coast. You can get roundtrip tickets from NYC to DC or Philly for $20, and Boston or Baltimore for $30. Each route has multiple bus operators and each operator has its own random street side pickup spot. Aka there is no bus station. Therefore, I recommend checking out www.chinatown-bus.org so you know where to catch each bus, find out how much it is, and even pre-purchase your tickets because sometimes that's the only way you can get on one of these crowded buses. Safety is not guaranteed. In fact the idea that your bus might catch on fire at any given moment might be kinda thrilling. Very kinda.

Bolt Bus: The Bolt Bus is pretty awesome. It's more spacious than Greyhound, has plug-ins for your electronics and even free Wi-Fi! Sure the connection might not be the best in the world, but you're on a bus hurtling down the highway for fuck's sake! Plus you can supposedly get $1 fares if you buy far enough in advance, but I'm pretty sure that's more of a gimmick. The only drawback to this bus line is that at the time I'm writing this (early 2011), Bolt Bus only services these cities: NYC, Boston, DC, Philly, Baltimore, a couple cities in Jersey, and a random train station in Maryland. They also fill up extremely far in advance because of the obvious reason that they are so much better than Greyhound. Get fares and schedules at BoltBus.com.

California Shuttle Bus: Since at this point, the high speed rail is only a faint fantasy, this sweet little dealie will take get you between SF and LA for only $25! Stephen Torres, one of the writers from BrokeAssStuart.com is the one who hipped me to it. Here's what he had to say:

> It's a pretty small time operation run by an older gentleman who answers the phones and tends to hop on the bus at some point during the trip to say hi and thank you for your patronage, peppering the patter with wisecracks. If you've ever traveled by bus in Mexico, it's kind of the same thing. The buses are usually in pretty good shape, have air conditioning/heat and the drivers are pretty good at getting the trip in under six or seven hours. They also have multiple drop off/ pick-up points as opposed to the scary terminal aesthetic. If that wasn't enough, you also get free entertainment. What trip would be complete unless it included being treated to such cinematic triumphs as *The House Bunny* or *Madea's Family Reunion*? The only downsides are that sometimes the details can be a little fuzzy, depending on how busy they are. If the passenger count was low, they would downgrade to a large van a few years back, which was a little awkward, but now it seems they cut days that they operate so it's best to call instead of just booking online. 877-225-0287. CaShuttleBus.com.

P.S.- To get the $25 deal, make sure to book in advance. Regular price is $35, with last minute at $40.

Megabus: Other than being the birthplace of such things as the Television (invented by John Logie Baird in 1929), Peter Pan (written by J.M. Barrie in 1904), and the cure for scurvy (some dude from Edinburgh in the 18th century), Scotland is also the far off land where Megabus got its start. Today you can catch one of these nice looking buses all over the Midwest, the Northeast and even Eastern Canada (ooh, how exotic!). All the coaches are equipped with free Wi-Fi and they apparently do that same $1 fare thingy that Bolt Bus does. Most are double-deckers, though, which may or may not freak some of you the fuck out. MegaBus.com

Trailways: Trailways is a group of over 80 independent bus companies that have all entered into an agreement to be under the same banner. It's kinda like the Rebel Alliance in Star Wars. I guess if we're gonna continue with that analogy, Greyhound must be the Empire, and all the little companies that comprise Trailways have banded together to try to pick off Greyhounds customers. But just like different factions in the Rebel Alliance, some bus companies are more badass than others. Certain vehicles would be the equivalent of the sleek and nimble Calamari Cruiser, while others are just as janky as whatever the fuck Ewoks use for transportation. You'll have to decide which is which. Trailways.com

And one more thing; Greyhound sucks because on trip from Philly to NYC, they searched my bag and took my Swiss Army Knife. Come on! What am I gonna do, crash the bus into the Empire State Building?

Driving

Despite being an anti-Semitic Nazi sympathizer (it's true–look it up), Henry Ford was a genius for bringing the horseless carriage to the people. Every time you're rolling down the street in your six-four you can tip your hat to him. What can I say? Even if Ford was a schmuck, being able to drive a car is pretty awesome. That being said, owning a car can be super-expensive (as I'm sure you very well know). Luckily if you decide to not own one, there are some great ways to use them without spending very much money.

Car Sharing: Owning a car in a city can be such a fucking hassle. I had a car in San Francisco for just one summer, and in that time I had it broken into once, towed once, and had scores of parking tickets. So I said to hell with it and got rid of it. Granted not having a vehicle isn't that big a deal if you're living in a somewhere like SF, New York, Chicago, or some other city that was big before the advent of the car. But realize, of course, that in a lot of cities a car is pretty much a necessity. That being said, car sharing may still be an alternative.

At this current moment, car sharing is defined by Wikipedia as "a model of car rental where people rent cars for short periods of time, often by the hour. They are attractive to customers who make only occasional use of a vehicle." O.K., Wikipedia is the source, so any of you jackasses can go change it to "Car sharing is where a group of guys circle-jerk onto a brand-new Mini Cooper with 20-inch rims, while a team of midgets in mustaches and sombreros flog each circle jerker with a standard-sized water hose." Then that will be the new definition of what car sharing is, and you should become a lot more cautious about signing up for it.

Regardless of how you choose to define it, car sharing is a great way to save money because you get rid of bills like insurance, gasoline that costs over $3 a gallon, and car payments. If you don't have a car but gotta run errands or just miss the feeling of rolling around with your friends and smoking a blunt, car sharing is perfect. Depending on where you live, there are different car sharing companies, and for each of them you have to pay an initiation fee, a small monthly fee, and an hourly usage fee. Some are non-profits and co-ops while others are clever capitalists. Generally, the co-op/non-profits charge for mileage as well. Many of the co-op/non-profits have deals set up so that if you belong to one (like City Car Share in the Bay Area) you can use another car sharing program (like Austin Car Share or Car Share Vermont) while visiting other cities. The ones with a "*" next to them in the list below are non profits or co-ops.

To find out more about car sharing (without having to think about Mini Cooper circle jerks) check out carsharing.net. Make sure you check out the "Where do they have it" page to see if there is one in your city. Here are some great options I've found.

*Ashland Car Share, Ashland, OR: Both loggers and hippies need cars sometimes. ashlandcarshare.com

*Car Share Vermont, Burlington: Is it me or are all of these car share things in hippie-ass places? carsharevt.org

*City Car Share, San Francisco: Need to pick up some medical marijuana in Oaksterdam before hitting the Mission for a burrito? City Car Share has you covered in the Bay Area. citycarshare.org.

City Wheels, Cleveland: For all those times when you wanna hang out in Cleveland. What? Lebron James used to do it. Do you think you're better than Lebron? mycitywheels.com

Community Car, Madison, WI: The main reason I wanna go to Madison is so I can then go to Wisconsin Dells, where there are more waterparks than anywhere else in the world. communitycar.com

Connect by Hertz: In many places throughout the U.S. (mostly at universities), the car rental giant is trying to get in on the car-sharing action. Personally, I think you should give your money to somebody else. connectbyhertz.com

Modo, Vancouver: Get your Canadian on while rolling in Vancouver, New Westminster, and Burnaby. I've been told that not all Canadians live in igloos, but I'm pretty sure that's a lie. modo.coop

*eGo Car Share, Denver: Neal Cassidy liked cars and was from Denver. I wonder if he would've used eGo Car Share. CarShare.org

Go Get Car Share, Australia: Yeeeah mate, this outfit will sort you out in Brisbane, Sydney, Melbourne, and Adelaide (those are in Australia, FYI). Just remember they drive on the wrong–I mean opposite–side of the road. goget.com.au

*HourCar, St. Paul, MN: The only things I know about the Twin Cities are Prince, Atmosphere, Brother Ali, Kirby Puckett, snow, and The Vikings. hourcar.org

*I-Go Car Sharing, Chicago: For when the El just won't cut it. igocars.org

*Ithaca Car Share, Ithaca, NY: I don't even know enough about this town to make a stupid comment. I think they have a college there or something. ithacacarshare.org

Kobenhavns Delebiler, Denmark: Copenhagen, bitches! And I'm not talking about the shit you put in your mouth. While the site is in Danish (once again not the thing you put it your mouth), they will respond to your emails in English. They probably speak it better than I do. koebenhavnsdelebiler.dk

*Philly Car Share, Philadelphia: Sure you can try Pat's and Gino's in the same trip, but if you wanna fit Jim's in there, you might need some wheels. phillycarshare.org

Mint, NYC: Who the hell drives in New York? drivemint.com.

U Car Share: You've used their parent company, U-haul, for all 70,000 moves you've made. If you're in a handful of places you can use this car sharing program, too. ucarshare.com

WeCar: WeCar is in many places throughout the U.S. (mostly at universities) and is the spawn of car-rental giant Enterprise. Personally, I think you should give your money to somebody else. This is just an example of a giant corporation getting on the "green" bandwagon strictly for profits. WeCar.com (more like "we car(e)" about getting your money).

Zipcar: Zipcar is fast becoming the Starbucks of the car sharing world, meaning you see the bastards on every corner. They are in 50-plus cities, even Los Angeles (yeah, I'm pretty confused about that one as well). I used Zipcar in SF for a while and really dug it. Then my lady got a car (and a parking space), so I got rid of my membership. But if she finally kicks me to the curb I'm totally gonna do car sharing again. Think about it, I could sleep in a different car every night of the week. zipcar.com

Car Rental: Getting cheap car rentals can be pretty tough, but there are a few things I can suggest. The first is to try booking through online travel bookers like Expedia, Hotwire, or any one of the myriad of others you can choose from. The other is to go straight to a car rental agency's website and see if they are having a promotion that might help you out. Also, whenever picking up your rental, make sure to ask the desk if there are any specials they've got going on or if you can get an upgrade. You never know how far a smile can get you.

O.K., so none of those were really great tips, but this one is. In fact it's so good, if we ever meet in person, you should probably try to get me laid. Or at least buy me a drink. Here it is: If you have a major credit card and you make a car rental reservation with it, the credit card company covers your rental insurance! Yeah, I know, that blew my mind when I found out, too. Just call your credit card company to double-check how much they cover (each is different), but seriously, I just saved you like 25 bucks a day. See—aren't you glad you bought this book now?

Thanks to Becky Shahvar from Keeping your Balance (keepingyourbalance.net) for the tip!

Get a Free Road Trip: If you've ever wanted to go on a road trip but couldn't for some reason (like don't have a car, or your car is a piece of shit and won't make it) you should look into Auto Driveaway. Basically what they do is take someone who needs their car transported someplace and connect them with someone to drive it there (possibly you). What a perfect match, right? The only connection I can think of that tops it is the combo of chocolate and peanut butter. Now that is what I call dynamite!

Anyway, here's how it works: you give them a $350 deposit that is returned to you when you safely deliver the car in the condition you picked it up in. They even give you your first tank of gas for free! You're only expected to drive 8 hours or 400 miles a day, and if you work it out with the agent beforehand, you might be able to negotiate extra time for sightseeing. It's a hell of a lot cheaper than renting a car. Check them out at autodriveaway.com.

An alternative to Auto Driveaway is HitTheRoad.ca. It's the same concept, really, but I'm pretty sure they pay for all the gas—meaning that it's a totally free trip for you. That being said, they have a bigger deposit. Theirs is $500 Canadian which at the time I'm writing this equals $473.82 American. Ain't that some shit? America Jr. is coming up! Did you know that the Canadian dollar is called the Loonie, and that the $2 bill is called the Toonie? Yeah, dood–Looney Tunes money. Anyway, if you do go with hittheroad.ca, tell them I sent you. They'll give me $50! Seriously.

Ridesharing: Ridesharing is kinda like the digital version of hitchhiking, but way less romantic (in a Jack Kerouac kind of way) and hopefully less stabby (in a deranged killer kind of way). There are multiple kinds of ridesharing, too. You can look for rides to various events, rides to work (just like carpooling to school except without my mom yelling, "I'm not starting this car until all of you have your damn seatbelts on!"), and, of course, rides to other towns. To get an idea of all the different ridesharing sites out there, just Google "rideshare." Or you can just do the Craigslist thing.

The only time I did a rideshare (other than getting hooked up with friends of friends) was when I caught a ride from San Francisco to Santa Cruz through craigslist. It was cool because the kid who drove me was doing this project where he would drive anyone pretty much anywhere, as long as he could film it. (it wasn't as craigslist-kinky as it sounds). He was doing a documentary on human interaction, and I think he ended up submitting the film to a film fest of sorts. Unfortunately my part didn't make it in because I was the first person he tried it on and the cameras weren't set up right. Wanna see it? Then go to coynedesignsf.com/testdriving.mov. It's pretty cool.

Hitchhiking: This is without a doubt the cheapest way to get from Point A to Point B, but it's also one of the most time-consuming, least reliable, and possibly most dangerous. I hitchhiked through most of western Ireland and a bit of Costa Rica. I also hitched every day of my sophomore year of college, but that was in Santa Cruz, CA. Anyone who's ever been there can attest to the fact that the rest of the U.S. does not work the way Santa Cruz does.

I'm actually quite bummed out by the state of hitchhiking in the US. If it wasn't looked at as such a dodgy proposition, I'd totally hitch everywhere. Shit, I like meeting interesting new people, and I like getting free rides. There was actually a time when it was totally normal and acceptable to hitchhike anywhere you needed to go (just read *On the Road* if you don't believe me). Unfortunately one or two psychos had to go and hack up the people they got rides from (or picked up), thus causing a media frenzy that made hitching in the USA looked upon as too dangerous. Fucking assholes.

Despite all this, though, hitchhiking is still something that can totally be done. I'm no expert, so if you're thinking about doing it check out some great tips at wikitravel.org/en/tips_for_hitchhiking and hitchwiki.org.

Travel By Sea

Cargo Ship: Don't worry, traveling by cargo ship has nothing to do with the 13 dead prostitutes in the second season of *The Wire*. Those girls were getting smuggled in. No one wants to smuggle your ass anywhere. Instead consider traveling by *cargo ship* as a broke-ass luxury cruise.

Now, it's not actually super-cheap; it can cost $80-$150 a day. I know—crazy, right? I thought it'd be like paying like 50 bucks to sleep on a pile of potato sacks and wash dishes for a one-eyed cook named Knuckles. But still, it's much cheaper than it would be if you were to take an actual cruise. The price includes your accommodations, your food, and maybe even a little something to drink. The food and accommodations are actually pretty nice: Many of the ships have swimming pools, and some freighters have gourmet chefs.

Another plus is that since it's a fucking cargo ship, you can bring as much luggage as you want—they've got plenty of room. Think about it like this: Let's say you gotta move to France or something and you wanna take all your crap with you. Going by ship is gonna be way cheaper than anything else because shipping all your belongs would cost thousands.

For a pretty in-depth guide on how do this whole thing check out seaplus.com

Sleeping on the Road

For ideas of where to sleep while traveling check out the chapter called Sleeping on page 59. What? Don't tell me you're too lazy to turn the pages, dammit!

Get Paid to Travel

Yup, there are ways to do this, but you're gonna have to flip to page 94 to find out what they are. Consider it like a scavenger hunt. (No, it's not actually like a scavenger hunt at all, is it?)

Broke-Ass Porn

Once a week at brokeassstuart.com we present Broke-Ass Porn. It's visually stimulating material for the financially impaired. If this shit doesn't get you going, you're not as broke as you thought:

Cheap Air Fare Websites

The other day I found myself sitting at the computer, playing with different cheap airfare sites, and fantasizing about buying a ticket. Oh yeah, it was hot. I even tweeted, "The most masturbatory thing I do is look at cheap airline tickets to random places in the world. Well, it's the second actually." Because, well, it sure felt a lot like mental masturbation.

And what's a bigger form of porn for a broke-ass than pretending you're in a position to buy a plane ticket to some exotic land? Seriously, travel is my biggest vice. Because of the nature of what I do, I occasionally get semi-substantial checks and the hardest thing is to not immediately go online and blow it all on a ticket. If that doesn't sound like the action of a junkie then I don't know what would.

Wanna join in on this ultimate form of broke-ass porn? Check out kayak.com/buzz. Now I know that most of the time you fly, you've gotta be some place at a certain time like your nephew's bar mitzvah or your ex's gender reassignment celebration. But if you have a job, I'm sure that you also get some vacation days. If you have some flexible time off and you wanna do some traveling, I suggest going to kayak.com/buzz. The way it works is that you plug in your nearest airport, the month you want to leave, and the region you want to visit, and it brings up the cheapest flights available. I just plugged in my info and found a roundtrip flight from San Francisco to Madrid for $590! Fuck....now I'm just teasing myself. If I had the time and money I'd so buy that ticket right now.

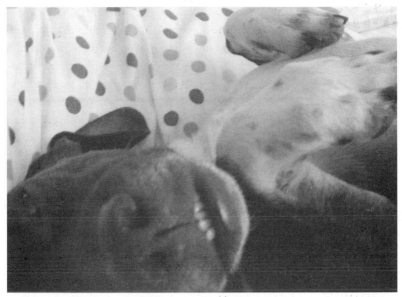

This is Detroit. I lived with him in Brooklyn. He's one of my favorite dogs ever, except that on the first day I lived there, he walked into my room, looked at me and then took a piss. I guess he was showing me who was the man of the house.

Sleeping

What do you want me to do, write a review of your future apartment? I can't do everything. What I will do, though, is give you some resources so you can help yourself find a place to sleep. If worse comes to worse, you can always sleep in a park.

Live like a refugee. If you bought this book, there's a good chance you already live in a shitty part of town. If you stole this book, you definitely do. But for those of you who got shit-canned after the economy fell apart, and are experiencing brokeitude for the first time: You should pay attention.

An easy way to save money on rent is to move where poorer people live. The rents there are bound to be cheaper. I'm not saying you should move to some horrible ghetto that's borderline post-apocalyptic, like you see in *The Wire*. I am saying that you should move to a neighborhood that rich people might be afraid to visit because they'd feel it was a little too "swarthy." A solid bet is to pick an area with a large population of immigrant families. There's not a lot of people who move out of their home country saying, "Man I'm so tired of being rich in (fill in a country), I'm gonna go be rich in the U.S. instead." Nope, not very common. Most people who move to developed countries do so because they're poor and seeking better economic opportunities. Often, the only places they can afford to live are the shittier parts of town. You should live where they live. An added bonus is that you'll be surrounded by all kinds of cheap and yummy ethnic food, interesting culture, and maybe you'll even pick up a new language. Unless you've got one of them lazy tongues.

Use Craigslist. If you're from the U.S. and you don't know about Craigslist yet, I'm pretty sure you're way beyond needing any of the help that this book can give you. But that's not the kind of shit my publisher wants me to say, so I'll write about it anyway.

Whether you are looking for a job, an apartment, the cute redhead you saw on the train, a used bike or simply some no-strings-attached oral sex, Craigslist has it all. This giant online bulletin board makes life so much easier. In fact, I've found all of my apartments there. Whatever…you already know all about the wondrous world of Craigslist, but I just have to tell you the best thing I ever saw posted. It was in the "missed connections" area for San Francisco and said, "Last night at King Diner I was the man who puked all over the place. You were the woman who helped me clean it up. I think I love you and want to see you again. That may be fairly easy because I'm pretty sure you are a prostitute. If you want to find me I'll be the guy at 5th & Market playing chess with the brown-bagged King Cobra 40." I'm not joking.

Live in a co-op. When I think of co-ops I generally think of two things. The first is the kind in NYC where rich people live that have all kinds of stupid rules and make the whole thing seem like kind of a bummer. The second is that kind that you find in college towns that are generally filled with hippies, punks, gays, dogs, gay dogs, and vegans and have a compost pile in the back. When I was in college there were numerous versions of this second kind spread throughout Santa Cruz, and they were generally either named after a progressive political leader or had an exclamation point in the name. Sometimes both. Since you can't afford the uppity, expensive kind of co-op, we're just gonna concern ourselves with the second kind.

Since everything at a co-op is communal it makes life a lot cheaper for everyone involved. All the residents chip money into a fund that goes toward buying things like household necessities (toilet paper, dish soap, shotgun shells) and food. Since you generally have like 25 housemates and everything is bought in bulk, both your rent and your living costs go way down.

Co-ops aren't for everyone, though. If you aren't into living with strange animals, tons of roommates, and hippies, you might want to pick a different kind of living situation. As for me, I think I could totally dig it as long as I didn't have to do shit that required concentration, like write this fucking book.

If you're interested in joining a co-op I'd recommend checking out the NASCO Guide to Co-Ops at nasco.coop/guide. They've got a full directory of co-ops in North America that can be searched by the kind you're looking for. They don't just cover housing, they also include things like media co-ops and health care co-ops.

Get down on a commune. I know you're picturing things like LSD, beards, girls with hairy armpits, and that scene in *Easy Rider*. But there's more to communes than just that. There's also group sex, if you're lucky.

While most of the communes that we think about from the '60s are gone, there are still hundreds of different kinds around the world today. They range everywhere from a group of fairly normal families who've decided to live together and share incomes to things like anarchist collectives and religious cults. What separates communes from co-ops is that in a co-op people share expenses, whereas in a commune they also share incomes. Seriously, some of them can be pretty freaky-deaky. To learn more and see a directory of communes around the world, go to the Fellowship of Intentional Community website at ic.org and click on "directory." It also lists ecovillages, co-ops, and cohousing.

Be a squatter. You've seen an abandoned building before, right? Ever thought of living there? That would be squatting. Squatting is the act of residing in abandoned or unoccupied places that you don't own. It's also a form of taking a piss or shit somewhere not in a toilet and generally outside, but that, my friends, is a subject for an entirely different book.

The legality of squatting is different in each country (US: illegal; UK: legal), so you have to be sure you bone up on the laws in your area and try to pick places that you're sure are no longer frequented. Getting arrested sucks. Trust me. Also, give the place a good look over and maybe even spend a night there to see how safe it is. It would be a major bummer if that shit were to collapse on you. How long you stay and whether you decide to put any work into the place is a call you'll have to make based on local laws and what you want from your squat. If you're looking at it as a short-term thing, don't worry about it too much, but if you expect to be there awhile (some squats have been around for decades), I'd say link up with some other people so you can make it a community effort. If you want some good step-by-step instructions on how to squat, you should look at wikihow.com/Squat-in-Abandoned-Property. Freegan.info also has good advice.

I actually saw Pierce Brosnan interviewed on the *Daily Show* once and he mentioned that at one point he lived in a punk-rock squat in London. Never would've expected that from such a fancy boy.

Sleep in your car. Depending on the size of your car, I'd look at this as a temporary solution. Sure it can be convenient, *kinda*, but it's certainly not ideal, and only a little more comfortable than sleeping on the sidewalk. If you decide to go this route for a longer period of time, try at least to trade or sell your car and get a van, RV, truck with a camper shell , or, at very least, an SUV. Unless you're extremely fastidious, you car will quickly be full of shit like clothes, sleeping bags, empty 7-Eleven Big Gulps, Burger King wrappers, and cheap pornography. It'll be like if your closet and your car had a love child. Yeah, nobody wants that.

Live in an RV. Living in San Francisco, you come to realize homelessness comes in many forms. There's more than just the guys who sleep on sidewalks and drink so much that you can see the piss puddle next to their passed out bodies. There's also the people who hustle just enough money to get a room each night at a seedy SRO hotel. Shit, there's even the kind of homeless where your roommate's boyfriend just came back from South America and needs a place to crash for 3 months while he writes his book. *Ahem*–yeah, I was that boyfriend (sorry once again, Jen and Abbey!)

As far as the not having a home thing goes, I think sleeping in a RV is pretty much ace. A couple months ago I was out at one of my favorite bars in SF, Doc's Clock, when a fan came up to chat with me about my books and shit. He told me that he was living in an RV in the Mission District because it was so much cheaper than renting. I was pretty surprised, since the kid was clean-cut enough for me not to realize he was a bum. Just kidding–he wasn't a bum, or even riff-raff for that matter; I think he actually had a job where he wore a button-down shirt everyday.

I see all manner of RVs parked on cutty side streets, so it seems to be working out for some people. As long as your vehicle actually turns on and can make it as far as the opposite side of the street (to avoid the street cleaning tickets), this isn't a horrible idea. The kid I talked to had a cheap membership to a nearby 24 Hour Fitness and just went there to shower each day. I'm sure the YMCA would also work, as would using various friends' showers until they got sick of you.

While I imagine it's probably pretty difficult to get someone to go home with you once you drop the "I live in an RV by the river" bomb, if you say it so it sounds like a joke you can probably play it off like you were misquoting Chris Farley all night. Then you just gotta hope that they're drunk enough to not care by the time you get "home."

I just did a quick search in craigslist's RV section and found one for as little as $1,000! So if you can come up with that much, then you've got yourself a new home, my friend.

Crash at an SRO. Ever read a Charles Bukowski book and wonder about the strange and squalid hotels he describes? Those are single room occupancy hotels–no-frills places that rent by the month, week, day, and sometimes hour, in generally seedy parts of town. More often than not, rooms don't have private bathrooms or kitchens, so those facilities are shared by an entire floor or sometimes multiple floors.

SROs can range from horrible places used mainly by addicts, prostitutes and the mentally deranged, to fairly nice spots that are better than most Super 8 hotels. If you're busted broke or in between apartments for bit, SROs can be a good bet, but you should ask to see a couple rooms before you decide to crash there. It will give you a good idea of who your neighbors will be and what the accommodations are like. We all have different breaking points when it comes to tolerating weird and wild shit.

A good friend of mine who was living in an SRO in SF actually brought a girl back there from a bar one night. I think the only one who wasn't impressed by this feat was the guy at the front desk. My buddy ended up having to pay double for the room that night.

Sleep with your mother. Mother Nature, that is. If sleeping out in the wilderness was good enough for your ancestors, it's good enough for you. Get yourself a tent and some camping gear (both can be found for cheap or free on Craigslist) and go sleep under the stars anywhere your little heart desires. Renting a campground will cost you a little bit of dough, but not everyone uses campgrounds. Go to downtown LA and see for yourself.

If you do decide that camping is the way for you, but don't want to pay the campground fees, the more remote a place you find the better. While cops in some cities don't really do anything if you're caught sleeping in the park (oh, the sweet beauty of San Francisco), police in other cities will fine you, arrest you, or both. I'm willing to bet Salt Lake City falls into the "both" category.

Another option is to sleep for free on Uncle Sam's property. The Bureau of Land Management (BLU) has a ridiculously large amount of acreage spread throughout the United States that it considers "underdeveloped." Since they aren't doing jack shit with it otherwise, you are allowed to camp there for free! Sweet, right? There are rules, though:

- You can only camp at that spot for 14 days, then you must move at least 25 miles away.

- Pack out what you pack in (this means don't leave your trash, asshole).

- Do not camp within 200 feet of any water source.

- Don't leave your campfire unattended.

- Keep non flammable things,cans and bottles, out of your fire.

- During high fire danger periods, no campfires are allowed.

• In general, be respectful of your surroundings. In other words, **don't be a fucktard.**

You'll need to bring your own supplies, including a way to purify your own water. I'm sure there are other rules, but those are the most important ones that I saw. Plus, I'm too lazy to write the rest out.

So where do you find these wild and magical places where the government will actually let you stay for free? In the middle of fucking nowhere. Seriously. At the very least, Uncle Sam is a shrewd, calculating, unfeeling business man without a conscience, so don't expect any of this land to be in Miami Beach. You know that if it's free, it's gotta be in a place where no one really wants to live.

To be honest, the best way to find your nearest free camping adventure is to Google *"dispersed camping"* and the name of your state. Since dispersed camping is what this kind of thing is called, and blm.gov doesn't make it easy to find the info (one big list would be nice), your Googling it will just make this whole operation so much easier. I don't have time to walk you through it on the phone. In fact, I'm currently trying to get that outsourced to India. *"Hello, this is Broke-Ass Rajiv. How may I assist you?"* In case you're a little slow and haven't figured it out yet, I'm going to tell you to Google a lot of things in this book.

If camping in the wilderness by yourself sounds a little too creepy, you can always try doing it with thousands of other people. Go to a Rainbow Gathering and eat mushrooms with more hippies than you can wrap your mind around or check out Burning Man for a week of ingesting chemicals and lots and lots of dust. Check out welcomehome.org and burningman.com to get more info on these absolutely amazing experiences. Neither of them are exactly cheap, but it sure beats getting eaten by mountain lions alone.

Move in with your folks. OK, let me start off by saying that I know not everyone can move back in with their folks. Some people's folks are just as broke or broker than they are. Other people have despicably hateful and demented parents who beat or molested them when they were kids. Some no longer have parents or grew up in foster care or worse. For those of you who fall into this category, all I can say is that I'm truly sorry that you do. That's some serious shit. While I'll probably make fun of you for a litany of reasons throughout this book, having a shitty home life while growing up isn't one of them.

But for the rest of you, don't be such fucking pussies. Assuming that your parents will let you do it, moving back in with them really isn't all that bad. Think about it like this: At first your folks will be so glad to have you back in the house, they might even do your laundry! Plus, you'll get free food, a free place to sleep (in your old room with your old Johnny Depp posters) and access to certain amenities only people's parents have, like boxes of Kleenex and dishwashers. Jesus Christ, having a dishwasher would be amazing!

While I don't know what your parents are like, they'll probably be stoked on you being there for at least a little bit. Chances are they like you a lot more than anyone else in the world does. They wanna see you do well and succeed. Sure, they might give you a little shit about it at first, but they probably miss you. Even so, they're still gonna want to you get a job so you can eventually move back out. Nobody wants to see their 27-year-old playing *Halo* in their underwear on the couch on a regular basis. So, while you might suddenly have more chores to do and won't be able to bring someone home from the bar, moving in with a parental unit is a good way to catch your breath and get your shit together while you get back on your feet.

It's fun to stay at the YMCA. Or, it used to be. I actually saw the Village People perform once, and it wasn't even that time I bumped my head and woke up in 1977. Growing up in San Diego, the big county fair was the Del Mar Fair (I think they've changed the name now), and all kinds of musical acts used to play there for free. Among others I saw Jewel, Foreigner, Steel Pulse, and yes, the Village People. It was very gay.

Truthfully, I don't think staying at the YMCA is as accessible to my generation as it was to previous ones. I always hear older people be like (in a creaky old guy voice), "When I first came to (fill in city here), I stayed at the YMCA until I was able to get a job and a place to live." Nowadays, hostels pretty much fill that role, and I've always imagined that the only people who crash at the YMCA these days are borderline homeless people. There's probably not a single gay Indian, cop, or construction worker sleeping at a YMCA as we speak. It's sad, I know.

For reals, though, there's about 30 or so YMCAs throughout the country that still have rooms to rent. Each one is individually priced and each has a different amount of space, so you might wanna call to see if it's right for you. In the New York City area, check out www. ymcanyc.org/ymca-of-greater-new-york/guest-rooms. Yeah, I know it's a long url. To find out if the Ys in your city rent rooms, go to ymca.net, click "About Us," then "Find Your Y." Contact the nearest branch and ask if they have guest rooms.

Sleep in a shelter, not on the street. When you're already broke, it only takes a handful of bad decisions to end up on the street. Luckily, there are charitable organizations like Saint Vincent De Paul, for example, that offer indoor sleeping accommodations as long as you follow their rules. These places also often have other resources at their disposal (like counseling and job placement services) to help you get back on your feet. To get a list of all the different homeless shelters in the U.S., check out homelessshelterdirectory.org.

Look into affordable housing. Depending on your income, you might qualify for some kind of housing subsidy. Yeah that's right, the government might have a little extra loot to help you afford a place to live. I'll let Betsy Crouch (aka Coach Sizzle), who you'll meet in the Financial section on page 199, break this down for you:

When it comes to rental assistance, what types of programs are offered by HUD (Department of Housing and Urban Development) and what do these terms really mean?

1. Privately owned subsidized housing: You rent a "regular" privately owned apartment, and the private owner receives money from the government to offer you a lower rent, i.e. the government helps you pay the rent.

2. Public housing ("projects"): Google "HUD Public Housing" and the name of your city or state to find your local public housing agency.

3. Housing Choice voucher program (Section 8): Use a voucher to pay for an apartment you find on your own.

Who is eligible for these programs? Low-income families and individuals based on:

1. Annual Gross Income

2. If you qualify as an elderly person, a person with a disability or as a family

3. US Citizenship/Immigration status

4. They check your references to see if you would be "good tenants"–better turn down your stereo.

5. Also they may deny those "whose habits and practices may be expected to have a detrimental effect on other tenants or on the project's environment." Uh oh.

What it takes to qualify differs in each city, so the best way to find out if you're eligible is to Google the name of your town and "affordable housing."

Move to Detroit. Considering the different places I've lived, my view of how much housing should cost is completely demented. For example, if you told me you bought a two-bedroom condo in Manhattan for eleven-million dollars, I'd probably be like, "Eleven-million huh? That sounds like a fair price." Seriously, with the shit I've paid just to rent a room in SF, you could rent a huge house for in most of the U.S. The cost of buying a place in SF or NY is so expensive and out of my reach that the numbers might as well be made up. So here's the thing: If you just can't afford where you live, move to Detroit.

I did some work with this girl who was originally from the Detroit area. One day she told me that she and her partner were going back to look at houses because they could buy one for–get this–$800! I mean, I knew Detroit was fucked, but really, a whole house for $800? That's just ridiculous! Apparently it costs the banks something like $2,000 to tear the houses down so they are just trying to offload them, hence the cheap price.

Now I know there's that part of you that just said, "Fuck the dumb shit, I'm buying two houses in Detroit. One for me to live in, and one to turn into an *exact replica* of Pee-Wee's Playhouse." But be warned that these houses are cheap because they're decrepit and almost certainly in a bad neighborhood. That being said, if you're handy and want to get in on the ground floor of what could be the next awesome urban movement (the Pee-Wee's Playhouse movement, of course), relocating to the Motor City might just be the thing for you. Just consider investing in a Kevlar vest. It will probably cost as much as your house.

Move to Kansas. Despite having issues with the theory of evolution being taught in its schools (yes, really), the state of Kansas might be the perfect place for you to move. Why? Because they are literally *giving away* land. Check out kansasfreeland.com. If you move to one of the 12 towns listed there they will give you land to build a house on. The only bummer part is that these towns seem to be in the middle of nowhere. I'm sure for some of you that's perfect, but I'd lose my mind. Unless…all of use move there and start our own little hedonistic playland. Holy shit, now we're talking! I'm thinking live sex shows, 24 hour bars, underground boxing matches, and shitload of water slides. You with me? That said, while the land is free, most municipalities require that you build a home with a foundation—not an RV, mobile home or tent—on the property within 12 months. (Thanks to the excellent writer Ethan Wolff for this tip.)

Get a sublet. Subletting is when you take somebody else's residence (a room or a full apartment/house) for a given amount of time while they are somewhere else. If you're one of those folks who doesn't have much or doesn't mind putting what they do have in storage, it's a great option. The least stressful way to go about it is if someone you or your friends know is looking to fill their spot. That way the whole thing involves far fewer strangers and you'll probably have some forewarning if your new housemates also happen to be speed freaks. Otherwise, Craigslist is the best option for finding sublets. If you only plan on being someplace for a short amount of time or just want something fairly stable while you weigh your options, subletting is perfect.

Crash at a college. While hooking up with hot collegiates is awesome despite cramming two bodies in one twin-sized bed, that's not what I'm talking about. If you live in a city with a big college population, you can usually rent a room in the dorm for really cheap during the summer. Also, a lot of kids are looking to sublet rooms in their places off campus when they leave for the summer as well, so start checking out Craigslist around a month before school ends.

Housesit a Mansion. Umm, how could this NOT be awesome? Finally, you can live like a millionaire without having to do the work it takes to be one. Trampoline rooms, here we come! And the best part is, you can do it for different properties all over the world.

The Caretaker Gazette (caretaker.org) is "a unique newsletter containing property caretaking and house sitting jobs, advice, and information for property caretakers, housesitters, and landowners." Basically, the way it works is that you pay $30 a year to get the bimonthly e-newsletter, plus you get access to the housesitting and caretaking jobs that are posted to the site daily. These are often people who need a position filled immediately. Shit, if you play your cards right, you can move from place to place living rent-free for a very long time. In fact, some places even pay! Check out this listing that I just read:

"LOOKING FOR a semi-retired person or couple for part-time light duties on a small Caribbean resort. Free housing on the resort's premises plus moderate pay in exchange for about 50 hours per month work. Applicant should be in good health, resourceful, and addiction and drug-free. If you are handy, it is a plus. Please email letter to..."

Did you read that?! Only 50 hours work *per month!* You should know though that most people don't let just any schmuck come over and watch their 15th century manor in the English countryside. I'm pretty sure you've got to provide some references and prove that you're a reasonable and responsible member of society. Unfortunately, that might be the hard part.

Hostels are not hostile. Ah yes, hostels. Where else can you stay so cheaply and meet cool, interesting people from around the world to have conversations, and possibly even casual sex, with? Let's just say that most hostel bathrooms have more DNA in them than an entire season of *Law and Order*; so be sure to wear flip-flops in the shower. But pursuits of the heart (or loins) aren't the only reason to bunk down in a hostel. You can also save a lot of money.

Hostels are far cheaper than staying in a hotel because they generally have dormitory rooms that sleep anywhere from three to16 people. If sleeping with earplugs doesn't work for you, never fear—most hostels have a few rooms they rent as singles or doubles. Some even have their own bathrooms. That way, you at least know who's been doing what in the shower. But there is more to the hostel experience than just a cheap place to crash. Even if you don't meet someone to swap fluids with, you'll certainly meet someone to swap stories with. I've made friends at hostels all over the world. In fact, I just got back from a wedding of someone I met in hostel in Dublin.

Kate Kotler (katekotler.com) recommends that: "If you're over the age of 25 and not a student, call the hostel instead of booking online. Most hostels have an 'international travelers or students only' policy, mostly to avoid having to refund grumpy old people." This mostly applies to hostels in the U.S.

Research and book hostels on sites like hostelz.com, hostels.com and hostelworld.com.

Be a swinger. While spouse swapping will never be as hip as it was in the '70's, house swapping is the new hotness for anyone who wants to stay in a place with all the comforts of home. You go to websites like homelink.org or sabbaticalhomes.com, where you connect with people from all over the world. When you find someone in the city you're trying to visit who also wants to visit your area, you can then arrange to stay in each other's homes. That way no one has to come out-of-pocket for lodging. Sweet, right? Just don't be surprised when Jude Law or Cameron Diaz don't show up (yes, I totally know you watched *The Holiday* so stop pretending like you don't get the reference), or when no one wants to swap with you because you live in a flophouse in the ghetto. Same goes if you live in Cleveland (Sorry, Grandpa).

Haggle with your landlord. Unless your landlord is Mister Burns from The Simpsons or some other rich bastard, chances are they feel the economic pinch almost as much as you do. And because of this, they'd rather keep you in your place than risk you moving out leaving them not being able to fill the space. You can use these circumstances to your advantage by being resourceful. It's pretty much what ninjas do all the time. You, my friend, are a recession ninja! Unfortunately, using a shuriken on your landlord isn't legal–or very cool of you–so you'll have to use strategy as your weapon instead.

First, it helps if you're a desirable tenant. This means having good credit and always paying rent on time. If you meet that criteria, start looking around at other spots in your neighborhood and comparing prices. Once you get together a list of places that are cheaper than yours, bring them to your landlord and say something like, "I really like living here, but these places are just cheaper and I'm considering moving." Make sure to remind them how good of a tenant you are.

If that doesn't work, the next step is to try bartering with them. See if your landlord will lower your rent in exchange for any skills you might have. (Being able to pound a tall boy faster than your friends doesn't count, by the way.) Are you good with PhotoShop? Maybe you can help your landlord design some new business cards. Are you handy? Offer to fix up some stuff. Are you a paralegal? Perhaps you can peruse some documents for them. Hell, if worse comes to worse, offer to do some janitorial work. Once you do come to an agreement, just make sure you get it in writing so the bastard doesn't try to pull a fast one on you later.

Also, like with any form of haggling, once the negotiations have begun, decide what your ideal price would be and overshoot the mark. For example, if you're looking to pay $700 a month, see if they will accept $500 and work your way up from there.

I hope this works for you, my little recession ninja!

Rent in the off-season. I always say I'm bicoastal-curious because, while I live in SF and spend a lot of time in New York, I don't actually live in both places (even though I wish I did). If you're like me and have mad love for more than one place, consider living in multiple ones. Pick places that have pretty significant, yet opposite, tourist seasons and then go live in these places during the off season. The rents in these places will be WAY cheaper when it's not tourist season so you'll be able to get a place for significantly cheaper than you would at other parts of the year. Plus, if you do decide you wanna stay around during the busy part of the year, you'll know all the locals by that time and will most likely be able to line up some well-paying seasonal work and decent priced housing.

Use airbnb.com. Using this site is a bit of a leap of faith for both parties involved, but great for staying in expensive cities or ones that might not be big enough to have hostels. Folks who have a spare room (or apartment, or sometimes even futon) post it up on this site to rent out. All the amenities (laundry, wireless, kitchen access, etc) are listed clearly—some even include free meals! You can read user reviews of past people who have stayed there, and it's good for you to make sure to get reviews of yourself as a tenant so they know you will not break all of their belongings or try to light them on fire in the middle of night. You might even make a friend to do a housing swap with in the future if you live somewhere they might want to visit. Learn more at airbnb.com.

Couch surf around the world. Whether visiting a buddy in another city or simply being too drunk to drive home, everybody has crashed on a couch before. Up until recently most couches crashed on belonged to a friend, a friend of a friend, or just a random person whose party you ended up passing out at (and having your face drawn on with marker). Thanks to couchsurfing.com, you can now find the discomfort of sleeping on a sofa anywhere in the world. Just log onto the site, create a profile, and start networking with like-minded travelers and couch owners in -cities you plan to visit. Of course, not all situations are gonna be ideal, but it's sure cheaper than a hotel. If you're worried about safety, the site has guidelines that outline a person's reliability based on the testimonials by their previous couchsurfees.

An alternative to CouchSurfing is globalfreeloaders.com. While it isn't nearly as good a website as CouchSurfing, it does have the same premise: staying with random people for free. One thing that GlobalFreeloaders.com stresses, though, is you that you gotta give to get. They encourage that for every person who lets you crash with them, you should let someone crash with you. It's kinda like Paul McCartney said, "The love you take is equal to the love you make." But with couches.

Another site in the same vein is usservas.org. U.S. Servas has been around for over 60 years, and their goal is to create "peace building" through international interaction. It differs from the CouchSurfing and GlobalFreeloaders.com in the sense that to be a member you have to pay a yearly fee of $50 if you want to use the service nationally, and $85 if you want to use it internationally. They also charge a deposit of $15 (national) and $25 (international) for the list of hosts. Not a bad deal considering there are over 15,000 of them throughout the world. I have a feeling, though, that most of the hosts are old hip people instead of young hip people.

A couple other sites where you can find free places to crash are bewelcome.org and hospitalityclub.org.

Couch Surfing Do's and Don'ts

Do: Bring some kind of gift, but make sure it's appropriate. While a GI Joe action figure will work for most people, some people just have no taste, so go with something safe–like booze.

Don't: Throw your shit everywhere. You're in someone else's living room, for Christ's sake. Try to make a neat little pile in the corner.

Do: Bring some sweatpants or something to sleep in. Nobody wants to see you walking to the bathroom in your skivvies (unless you're hot, of course).

Don't: Get so drunk that you piss yourself on the futon. Seriously, some guy did that at my house once. What the fuck?

Do: Pay for whatever you ruin if you do happen to piss yourself, even if you gotta buy a new futon (which that guy actually did).

Don't: Criticize your host's cleanliness or living environment. You're no prize either.

Do: Try to graduate from the couch to the bed if the situation allows. Getting laid and sleeping in a bed is better than masturbating in the shower and sleeping on the couch. Feel it out first, though, so you don't become the creepy person sleeping on the sidewalk.

Don't: Overstay your welcome. Always keep your options for other couches open and be ready to hop. You don't want your host to get sick of you.

Broke-Ass Porn

Once a week at brokeassstuart.com we present Broke-Ass Porn. It's visually stimulating material for the financially impaired. If this shit doesn't get you going, you're not as broke as you thought:

Street Furniture

Oh, street furniture, how you break my heart. There was a time in the not-too-distant past where you could pick up pretty much any furniture from the street and bring it into your place of residence. Barring instances of rain, most furniture you found was in decent enough condition to reasonably become part of your living room. Then bed bugs came back with a vengeance. Yes, bed bugs have virtually ruined one of the main ways I've been able to afford furnishings.

A little bit ago a friend of mine wrote an article in the San Francisco Bay Guardian about the resurgence of bed bugs in the United States. I'm not gonna go into detail about it because that's his job, but you should Google the article and read it if you're as despondent about the loss of street furniture as I am.

Don't get me wrong, there are still some things you can get off the street, like the awesome '60s pea-green lamp we found (pictured above), but you have to be very careful. Bed bugs suck—trust me—and just one hopping a ride on the used recliner you found can render everyone in your building itching and possibly homeless. Wow, I guess this wasn't really isn't a Broke-Ass Porn as much as it is a Broke-Ass Mourn. Sorry about that, folks.

Is there a classification for purchasable items that ranks below "chachkies?

Shopping

Look, when you don't have any money, spending what little you do have sucks. But hell, we all have out needs; some of them weirder than others (you know who you are). So below are some tips on how to get what you need with out without making your wallet bleed.

Apple Discount: I made the switch to Mac a couple years ago, and I've gotta tell you, I'm never going back. My Mac is SO much better than any PC I've ever had. If you're ever considering making the switch, go talk to someone in the store to figure out exactly what you want, and then buy it online. If you do that, you can get the student discount by just clicking a box that says you're a student. They never verify this. This student discount gives you 10-15% off, depending on the item. Not bad right? I'm not sure if you can do the same with other Apple products, because I haven't tried, but I don't see why you wouldn't be able to.

Also, I know that some bigger corporations get certain small (like 4-7%) discounts as well. Who's to say you don't work at one of those? Go into the Mac store one day and try to find out which companies get these discounts. Then next time you buy something in there mention that you work at said company. Then let the discounts rain down like dollar bills in a strip club.

Fucking IKEA: I'm going to preface this by saying that I hate the fucking IKEA store. In fact from now on every time I mention the fucking IKEA store I'm going to call it the "fucking IKEA store." Why? Because going to the fucking IKEA store is single handedly the easiest way to get into a fight with your significant other. And if you live together, well...one of you is most likely gonna end up sleeping on the couch that night. That's just the way it is.

Despite my absolute loathing of the fucking IKEA store, the furniture created by the Swedish company has played a role in many of our lives. It's like you outfit your first couple apartments in hand-me-downs and shit from the Salvation Army and then for your third or fourth one you add a few brand new items to your furnishings. These are almost always from IKEA. Maybe not from the fucking IKEA store (one may not be by your house), but certainly from online. This you're already aware of. Right now you're probably like, "No shit Sherlock. You just described everybody I know." Well here's my point: you don't need to buy brand new IKEA gear any more.

First of all, that shit is not built to last. I mean, it's pretty much a known fact that all of IKEA's furniture is made by Smurfs, and we all know that those little bastards are generally way too fucked on drugs to build anything correctly.* Anyone who lives in a house made of mushrooms can't be counted on to be reliable at any job. Secondly, if you really want some IKEA stuff, get it on Craigslist. Craigslist's furniture section is virtually drowning in things from IKEA. Why buy it new when you can buy it used? And the third and most important thing is that IKEA Hackers (ikeahackers.net) exists. This site is fucking brilliant! It gives you step by step instructions on how to MacGyver the hell out of tons of different IKEA furnishings in order to let them reach their full potential. It teaches you how to make things like: lamps out of watering cans, pinhole cameras out of potholders and speakers out of salad bowls. Awesome sauce!

OK not really, but the furniture still sucks.

So here's what you should really do next time you need furniture: Once you decide what you're looking for, go to IKEA Hacker and see what kind of suggestions they have for what you want. It's pretty poorly organized, but after a little bit you'll get the hang of it. Then go to Craigslist and buy the necessary Swedish-named piece, bring it home, and then get to work. Now you never have to set foot in the fucking IKEA store again!

Big ups to Laura Smith the NYC editor for BrokeAssStuart.com for hipping me to this!

99 Cent Stores: By nature, being a broke-ass can be quite limiting, especially when it comes to buying things you actually need. For example, as much you may want one of those amazing looking Dyson vacuum cleaners for your house, you end up getting the used $25 one from the Salvadorian junk shop on 24th St. And that's why 99 cent stores are the shit. There's something amazingly sexy about being able to walk into a place and say to yourself, "Holy shit! I can afford everything in here!" It's like suddenly being transformed into Jay-Z for 20 minutes. I think from now on, I'm only going to buy people's birthday presents at 99 cent stores, and it's gonna awesome. My buddy's birthday is coming up and I've decided to get him a hammer, some nail clippers, a highly flammable stuffed animal, and a 12-pack of toilet paper. Why? Because it'll only cost me $5 and it's all useful stuff. Do you think they do gift wrapping? Just one thing: although I feel that the 99 cent store is great for almost everything, one thing it is not is pregnancy tests. Like, seriously. Just the mere fact that they're usually placed in the gum/candy/tape/ impulse buy aisle means they are not to be trusted, even if they are marked up to a $1.99 to show "quality."

Police Auctions: You know what happens when cops confiscate the possessions of people they catch? They sell that shit. Well not immediately. First they use it for evidence and after they are done with that, the owner has about 90 days to pick it up. After that it gets auctioned off. I'm talking about things like cars, boats, jewelry, art and just about anything else you can think of. This means that you can score pretty big. It used to be that police auctions happened in person, but nowadays they are doing that shit online. Check out sites like PropertyRoom.com and PoliceAuctions.com. Gov-Auctions.org is great if you're just looking for a vehicle, although it's not for the indecisive since you can't do much more than look at it, sniff inside, and then decide if you want to bid or not. Be aware: there is no return policy. Truthfully though there are tons of sites to choose from—use the Internet to find what your local area has to offer.

Swap Meets/Flea Markets: Swap Meet, Flea Market, call it what you will. Regardless, they're the same all over. While I'm sure the wares might be different at swap meet in rural Vermont than one in Salt Lake City, the concept is still the same: bargain your ass off, motherfuckers. What I like about swap meets is the wide range of quality and vendors present. Sure there's the cute elderly gay couples who sells shit like art deco coffee tables and vintage lamps, but there's also the crazy Vietnam Vets who sell army fatigues, bayonets, and switchblades, and can probably also get you live grenades if you know how to ask them. At least that's how the one I used to go in the San Diego Sports Arena's parking lot was. Most of the vendors there were just a half step and four missing teeth away from being Carnies.

Free Smell Goods: I used to be a cologne junkie, I even collected the stuff. It's weird, I'd be walking around town in clothes that cost less than $70 (including shoes) but I'd be rocking $50 cologne. Apparently even broke-asses have their little vanity vices.

I'm not sure you know this or not, but you can get perfume/cologne for free. Just go to a department store (or Sephora), pretend like you might want to buy some fragrances, and then ask them if they have some samples. They always do, and they will give you tiny take home bottles for free. So please STOP smelling bad. This is the 21st century. You know who you are.

Pro Tip:

Wanna get all kinds of nice stuff for free? Figure out when school ends at any private universities nearby. A lot of the kids that go to these schools come from money and their parents buy them top of line stuff for their dorm rooms. Since rich kids figure that daddy will just buy them a new leather ottoman next year, they'll just throw away all the stuff they aren't gonna bring back to their parents homes. So, if you figure out when all the freshmen are moving out, you can score some really dope goods just sitting on the side walk or out by the dumpsters.

How to Dress Yourself

Just because you're broke, doesn't mean you can't look fly. Below are a few pointers to help you in that direction. But up top, let me just put this one out there: taking a shower is the first step. Because if you're stinky, it doesn't matter how good you look.

H&M, Forever 21, etc: Big chain stores that sell reasonably priced fashionable clothes...hmm...should these even be in here? I guess so cuz they're cheap but...well...you know how you try to shop ethically, supporting independent business and not buying sweatshop made clothing, but at the same time you are totally broke but also want to look good? I guess these stores fully encompass that dilemma.

Keep Your Cheap Basics Cheap: Buying an Armani undershirt has to be one of the stupidest things I can think of. It's a goddamn undershirt, no one is gonna see it. A good way to cut costs on clothing is buy cheap basics. Get your socks, underwear, undershirts, camisoles, tank tops, and other such things from brands you've never heard of. If you're in a big city you can get these things at mom and pop stores in discount shopping areas (like Chinatown), and if you're out in the burbs you can always hit up a big chain store like Walmart (only if you have to). Then just have a few pairs of them good looking undies for nights when you think you might actually be scoring.

Keep it Simple: One of the easiest ways to look good and shop cheaply is to buy clothes with simple interchangeable colors. Figure out what hues look good on you and then get some plain tops in a few shades of those colors. A simple grey t-shirt and a pair of jeans is absolutely classic and looks good on both men and women. Same goes for black clothing. Get a pair of black jeans and a plain black shirt, and not only could wear them every day without your friends noticing, you'll look good the whole time too! Especially if your friends are bling.

Accessorize: Look, I'm no style maven, but I'm a pretty well dressed dude considering how little I spend on clothes. Here's the key: accessorize, and I'm not talking about going to Claire's in the mall and getting a different scrunchie to match every shirt you own. It's the little things that make an outfit. Get a cheap golf cap in a thrift store, or some buttons of your favorite bands, or a three-finger ring, or a well patterned scarf, or even a crazy belt buckle. By adding these types of things to an outfit that previously consisted of a simple shirt and jeans, and suddenly you're stylish.

Be Wary of Anything Wildly Popular: Those are words I try to live by. Pretty much anything that is wildly popular will only remain so for a very short while. Take Justin Beiber for example. At the time I'm writing this he's an incredibly famous teenage boy who looks like a young lesbian, and probably fucks gorgeous women 10 years his senior. He better enjoy it while he can, because chances are he'll be giving BJs for crack money sometime in the next five years. Well, maybe not, but you know what I mean. Nothing stays popular forever. This same thing applies to clothing. You know what was wildly popular just a couple years ago? Ed Hardy gear. And you know who wears it now? Total fucking douchebags. Buying whatever clothes are popular at the moment will not only be costly, but in just a few years you'll be left with a closet of clothes that just look stupid. Fuck fashion. Fashion is for people who don't have any style. Dress your own way.

Be a Thrift Store Whore

Why pay top dollar for new clothes when you have decades of used clothes to choose from?

Don't Believe the Hype: Not all used clothing stores are created equal, and finding great deals requires knowing which store is which. To begin with, avoid any place that sells "vintage" clothing because "vintage" is just another name for expensive, and who wants to pay a load of money to wear someone else's clothes? Same goes for "consignment". Then there are stores that sell "second-hand" or "used" clothing. The prices in these places can go either way, so make sure you check out a few tags before you invest too much time. What you're really looking for are thrift stores because, well…they're called thrift stores. Every town has them and while some act as nationwide charities and institutions (Salvation Army, Goodwill), others are simply local businesses that provide cool, cheap threads.

Patience Young Padawan: One of the first things you need to know about thrifting is that it requires patience. Oh sweet lord does it require patience. But as a very wise bottle of ketchup once said, "Good things come to those who wait." Sometimes you can spend an hour looking in a thrift store before you find something that you want, but generally speaking, the things you do find are often amazing (not to mention cheap). One way to speed up the process is to thrift with a purpose. Think of a particular way you want an outfit to look and either wear or bring in the pieces that you already have. That way you can immediately see if the $5 floral polyester shirt you're holding will actually go with that leisure suit you so desperately love. Luckily, if you buy it and don't like it, you can always sell it back to them.

Get out of Dodge: One of my favorite things to do when I'm in random places is to check out their thrift stores. All the joints in places like San Francisco, New York, and Los Angeles are already pretty picked through. So when I find myself in far-flung places like El Paso or Bellingham, those are the cities I find the best scores in. But there's no need to go that far; just go to a small town outside your city and I bet you'll find something good.

A Gift Economy

A lot of people hear Gift Economy and automatically think of the questionably enthusiastic people standing in public places with signs for "Free Hugs," which you probably avoid since little good usually comes from smooshing up against a stranger. The movement, which is based on the idea of giving or doing good without expecting anything in return, usually has the most to do with fuzzy feelings inside but below I'm going to tell you how you can get more than a snaggletoothed smile from a creepster on the subway platform.

The Really Really Free Market: The RRFM is like a broke-ass holiday where everyone gets a present. Think of it as Christmas but you don't have to buy people stuff they don't want, look at stupid snowman sweaters, or end up getting drunk and screaming, "Fuck you dad! You don't even know me!" The way it works is that everyone brings a bunch of stuff they want to get rid of to a central place like a park. Then they lay it all out and give it to whoever wants it. To quote an esteemed scholar named wikipedia, "It holds as a major goal to build a community based on sharing resources, caring for one another and improving the collective lives of all. Markets often vary in character, but they generally offer both goods and services. Participants bring unneeded items, food, skills and talents such as entertainment or haircuts." If free stuff is something you're into (and I know it is) find out where your nearest RRFM is by going to ReallyReallyFree.org and clicking on "Other RRFMs". They have them all over the country and in other countries like Australia and Brazil. They even have one in Flagstaff, Arizona! I didn't know they tolerated that kind of anticapitalist shit in Arizona.

Free Stores: Yeah, I know that sounds like a contradiction but there really are such things as free stores. They are places you can visit and then go home with pretty much anything not nailed down, for free. I visited one in a squat I hung out at in Madrid. As far as I know the first free store was started by the Diggers in San Francisco's Haight-Ashbury district in the 1960's and now there are a respectable number of them throughout the world.

Before you get all crazy and start running around and screaming like some lady with rollers in her hair who just won a Sea-Doo on the Price is Right, I'm gonna warn you that you're not gonna be finding expensive designer clothes at the free stores. Luckily you're not into that anyways. Right? The stuff you do find there is gonna be more on a garage sale kind of wavelength, but hey, did I mention it was free?

Look, capitalism is pretty fucked up. It's got us all chasing our tails and trying to feel complete by consuming products we don't really need. Free stores are a reaction to this. While some require you to drop something off every time you pick something up, most of them just let you have what you want. At the time I'm writing this there are free stores in Maryland, Michigan, Ohio, Massachusetts, Colorado, Oregon, and in foreign countries like Germany, Spain, and the Netherlands. To find the one nearest you, go to the wikipedia page about "give-away shops."

How to Get FREE Anything: The Freecycle Network (FreeCycle. org) is a network of nearly 8 million people devoted to keeping good stuff out of landfills and in circulation. Their mission statement says, "Our mission is to build a worldwide gifting movement that reduces waste, saves precious resources & eases the burden on our landfills while enabling our members to benefit from the strength of a larger community." Consider it a digital version the Really Really Free Market (remember that thing I talked about two pages ago?).

The way Freecycle works is that you go to the site, plug in where you live, and then join the Freecycle network nearest you. At the time I'm writing this, all the Freecycle networks are yahoo groups where people post a message describing what they have to give or what they're looking for. Then other members in the community can respond. It's a good way to get pretty much anything. You can find anything from lunch boxes to refrigerators to books to clothes. Unfortunately no plants, animals or small children are allowed to be given away. And the best part is that it only costs $3000 to sign up. Nah, I'm just fucking with you, it's totally free! All the things you get or give through Freecycle are 100% free with no strings attached.

Some other sites that have similar goals are: FreeSharing.org, OnlineRecyclers.com and free-economy.org. Who said there was no such thing as a free lunchbox?

To find out more about gift economies and to stay up on all the new places that pop up, you should go to wiki.gifteconomy.org

Swapping Stuff

Whether it's a VHS tape of Riding in Cars with Boys or the juicer you bought before you realized what a bitch it would be to clean, you probably have stuff lying around you really don't want or use anymore. Well, so does everyone else, so the following section lists sites designed for swapping your wares with someone else. It's not free like the previous section, but you'll likely have a larger selection to choose from since folks will post things others would actually deem worthy of trading (you didn't try to trade a bag of prunes in the lunchroom did you?). There are lots of other trading sites out there, but I've listed the ones that don't charge you money.

Media Mail: Before you read the stuff below about how you can swap your old crap for someone else's, you should also know that if you're sending books, dvds, cds or any other media by mail, that you should make sure to ask for the media mail price. Media Mail was set up so libraries could trade books without having to pay exorbitant prices for shipping. Now, according to USPS.com, "Media Mail® service is a cost efficient way to mail books, sound recordings, recorded video tapes, printed music, and recorded computer-readable media (such as CDs, DVDs, and diskettes). Media Mail cannot contain advertising except for incidental announcements of books. The maximum weight for Media Mail is 70 lbs." How cool is that little "®"? I want to put it after a term I coined, like "furplunkt." I'm defining it as being WAY too fucked up like, "Man I was SO furplunkt® last night that I woke up without pants in my neighbor's kiddy pool spooning a lawn chair. Anyways, check out Media Mail!

Trade Media: Swap (Swap.com) is badass! It's an online community where you can trade books, music, dvds and video games with other users all over the US. The way it works is: you list the stuff you wanna trade and the stuff you're looking for by entering the numbers on the barcode. Then the site instantly lists thousands of items you can get for what you're offering. You then pick one, and the site makes up a shipping label for you to print out which includes the cost and weight. You can either pay for your shipping through the site or by going to the post office. Amazing, right!? It's like, why would you even buy any of these forms of media again? And the best part is that the Swap website is super functional, smart, and easy to use. If only you could do this for mail order brides, I'd never leave my house.

Swap Zines: Zines will always hold a dear place in my heart because that's how I got my start. I still collect zines actually, so if you've made one I'd love for you to send me a copy. In fact, I'll send you some stickers in exchange. Hit me up at info@BrokeAssStuart.com for that.

If you're into trading zines for other zines though, I recommend ZineSwap.com. Based in London, the way Zine Swap works is that you send them 3 copies of your zine, along with a self addressed envelope, and then they send you somebody else's zines back. It's as simple as that! I've got some leftovers of my own zines actually now that I think about it. Maybe I'll give it a try.

Trade Books: Books can be expensive sometimes, especially if you buy them new. That's why BookMooch.com is sweet. The way it works is: 1) Type in the books you wanna giveaway. 2) Receive requests from others for your books. 3) Mail your books and receive points. 4) Ask for books from others with your points. I'm not quite sure how all this "points" mumbo-jumbo works out and I'm too lazy to read more from their website, so you'll have to check it out for yourself. But hey, at least you don't have to buy any books for awhile....oh wait, please keep buying mine though. I'd really like to reach my goal of having a butler to verbally abuse. I'd call him Bentley or something else British-sounding like "Sterling" or "Queen Elizabeth" and throw my shoes at him when I got drunk and angry. Just kidding! Kind of.

Exchange Textbooks: I've always thought that the entire textbook industry was a complete shakedown. I remember trying to resell a textbook after finishing a Spanish class in college, and the bookstore refusing to buy it back because the company was printing a new edition the following year. I'm still pissed about that. I mean really, a new edition of a Spanish book? This isn't astrophysics, it's not like they've discovered new fucking Spanish since the last book was put out! But anyways now there's a way to get around some the ridiculous costs of buying textbooks. TextSwap.com allows you to swap books with students at tons of different universities. Now hopefully you'll have more money to go out and get totally furplunkt®.

Recycle Your Clothes: This one is for the ladies, and the fellas who like to wear ladies clothes. I say this not because chicks like to shop more than guys who aren't drag queens (though this is true) but mainly because most of the clothes on clothes swapping sites are women's clothes. Hell, even a majority of the men's clothes being swapped are being put out there by women who've raided their man's closet. Addiction makes us do unfair things to the ones we love, even an addiction to clothes swapping.

There's a bunch of different clothes trading sites and each works better for different people. So here is a list of some of the ones that are free and you can decide which one you like best: BigWardrobe.com, RehashClothes.com, and DigNSwap.com. Also, if you've got kids, all this clothing swapping can be awesome because those little fuckers grow fast and are constantly in need of new gear.

Something you can do on your own is organize a clothing swap with a bunch of your friends. Pick someone's home who has lots of space, then tell a bunch of friends to come over with some drinks to share and all the clothes they wanna get rid of. After all the swapping is done, the leftover clothes can be given to charity.

Trade Everything: Sure swapping stuff like books and dvds is awesome but you can actually trade pretty much anything in your crappy apartment for stuff in other people's crappy apartment. Just check out U-exchange.com where everything from toys to luggage to electronics to various services are up for tradesies. People even set up housing swaps through U-Exchange. The website itself is pretty mediocre in terms of its design, but I guess the cats who run it aren't exactly making money off you trading your weird He-Man action figures for someone else's My Little Pony dolls.

Some other similar sites are TradeStuff.com, SwapAce.com, and SwapTreasures.com.

Broke-Ass Porn

Once a week at brokeassstuart.com we present Broke-Ass Porn. It's visually stimulating material for the financially impaired. If this shit doesn't get you going, you're not as broke as you thought:

Books

I'm a person of minor obsessions. I mean, I'm not the kind of cat who has every song ever created by The Grateful Dead, but when I find something I like, I get pretty into it for a little while. Right now my two obsessions are Law and Order (any of them, really, but SVU is my favorite) and Anne Rice's *The Vampire Chronicles.* In the past two weeks I've read Interview with the Vampire and the The Vampire Lestat. Now I'm already diving pretty deeply into *The Queen of the Damned* (which is fucking excellent so far). At least this is one of my healthier obsessions, unlike my obsession with trying to find the rumored midget hooker in the Tenderloin neighborhood in San Francisco (I've heard that when a car pulls up she hollers, "Half price!" I'm not kidding.).

But back to books. They might be the ultimate Broke-Ass Porn—wait, actually, pictures of tons of money is, but books are the attainable kind of Broke-Ass Porn. First of all, they are free (this crazy place called the library lets you borrow them) and they can also be all-consuming, so that you don't even want to go out and spend money. For example, I'm a bit hungover today (surprise, surprise), so instead of doing something like shopping for Hanukkah presents, I'm gonna lie around on the couch and read. That shit is FREE! If that's not sexy, I don't know what the hell is.

mike force

Making Money

Want some good ideas on how to get a job? Well luckily you've come to the right place. Uncle Broke-Ass here has got what you need, now all you have to do is not fuck it up. Happy job hunting sucka!

Craigslist: Do I really need to go over this one again?

General Job Hunting: Because of the many vagaries of life, finding a job can be fucking hard, especially in this shitty economic climate. Of course there's Craigslist but you are competing with every other jobless chump out there. If you're just looking for a job that's retail or food service or anything else that doesn't require a particular degree, what I always suggest is this: pick a neighborhood and dress accordingly. If you are going to an uppity part of town, dress like you're meeting your significant other's parents for the first time and it's gonna be at a nice restaurant. If you are going to a young, hipper part of town dress like you did that one time when you tried out to be on *The Real World*. Make sure to bring out like 20 resumes a day and try to get rid of all of them. There will be a bunch of places that say, "Oh, we're not hiring but you can leave a resume." If you like the place, leave one, I've been called like three months later and you just never know. Ya know?

Get a Temp Job: The only office job I've ever had was an internship at Bill Graham Presents when I was 21. Considering that BGP is one of the biggest concert promoters in the Bay Area, it wasn't exactly a typical office job in the sense that I had a Mohawk for part of the time I was there. Needless to say, I don't have a lot of office experience, but if you know how to read, type, and file stuff, I know you can get a job as a temp. Find out what temp agencies are in your town and give them a ring. They'll probably interview you to see what your qualifications are and then help you find a temporary gig an office somewhere. They're kinda like pimps for paper pushers.

Be a Runner: Heidi Smith, one of writers for BrokeAssStuart.com recently did a piece on **TaskRabbit**. While it's currently only in Boston and San Francisco, there's a pretty good chance that it will be expanding to a city near you:

Task Rabbit is an online service where people can post those errands they don't have the time or skills to do themselves. Instantly, a post can then be viewed by hundreds of runners or "rabbits" (like me) that are eager to help someone complete a task. Think of it as an eBay service for running errands. The runners then bid a price on the task. The one with the task will immediately be notified and can then either accept, deny or counter offer the bidder's price. Once a runner is chosen, they will complete the task, close it out online, and then get paid electronically into their Task Rabbit account.

Just who are these runners, you might be asking? All of the runners have to go through a three-step application process before they can be a part of Task Rabbit. There is an online application, a phone screening and a background check in order to make sure some creep isn't coming over to do your laundry. You can also research the runner's profiles on the site to see which one seems most suitable for your task. Genius, right?

As a runner, I have done about eight tasks so far. I've delivered flowers to some guy's girlfriend, done research for another guy's blog, and worked a few bartending/catering gigs. The last one was so awesome – I helped a woman cater a party in her fabulous North Beach loft with the best view of the city I have ever seen. She was really cool and told me to eat and drink whatever I liked and to mingle with the guests. I worked it with another runner, who turned out to be really cool, and we even exchanged numbers after the gig was done. So I had a great time – and I got paid $80 to hang out for a few hours. Top that!

Be a Mystery Shopper: While I don't know if you actually get paid much to be a mystery shopper, you do get free stuff out of it. Basically, retail companies or restaurants that wanna snoop around and see if their employees are fucking off will contact a mystery shopper company. Then the company sends in someone to pretend to be a customer and secretly test the employee. I used to work at a mediocre Italian restaurant that was a chain in California. They use to have mystery shoppers come in every once in awhile and then a few days later we'd get a report. IF the report was bad enough, you could lose your job. Truthfully, I think it's a pretty shitty way to run a business because your employees end up fearing you instead of loving and respecting you. But then again, most big corporations don't care about their employees anyways. So, wanna get free food and gear in exchange for ratting on someone? Then check out SecretShopper.com, Volition.com, and MysteryShop.org.

Be a Babysitter: Just because you're not in high school anymore doesn't mean you can't make a little money babysitting. Not only do you get paid for hanging out and watching SpongeBob (he's totally awesome by the way) parents often dig into their pantries and fridges. So not only are you making money, you're getting fed too! What's that? You don't know anyone with kids? Never fear! Just check out SitterCity.com and sign up to be a babysitter. Just pass the screening process and you're on your way.

Teach English: If you're reading this there's a very good chance that you speak English. If in fact you don't speak English, and you can understand all this, you are a mind blowing creature of immense intelligence and I'm the one that should be asking you for advice. Most likely though, you fall into the first category, and this means that you have one amazingly marketable skill: the fact that you speak

English. See you're not completely useless.

Since English is the international business language, there are a lot of people out there willing to pay good money to learn how to speak it. This means that you can potentially get some work either in your home country or abroad. The first thing you gotta do is get a Teaching English as a Second Language (TEFL) certificate. Unfortunately this is gonna cost you a little bit of money; online courses start at $150. The good news though is that after finishing the course, many of the schools can help you find a job. There are literally hundreds of different TEFL training courses online and some are better regarded than others so you will probably have to do a little research into it yourself to decide which is the one for you. Just google "TEFL Certification" to get the ball rolling. Who knows, a year from now you might be teaching English in Thailand or tutoring some business folks in your own town.

Tutor or Give Lessons: Are you smarter than a 5th grader and not a registered sex offender? Then there's work out there for you! Figure out what you can possibly tutor or instruct someone in and then post some flyers at local coffee shops, rec centers, school bulletin boards, and wherever else people read things not on the Internet. Also try Craigslist. Craigslist is also a good place to research how much other people are charging for the same service you're offering. That way you will know how much to charge. You might be really good at math, but no one is gonna pay you $100 an hour to tutor their 10 year old.

Write Papers for Students: As far as I know, plagiarism isn't illegal, it's just unethical and ethical is a pretty bendy term anyways. Are you good with the English? Then sell your old papers or write new ones for current students. If you're this hard up for cash, you've probably got some extra time on your hands anyways, might as well put that $30,000 liberal arts degree to use. Just remember to have the kid show you a couple of his or her previous papers so you can see how bad they suck. That way nobody gets in trouble when you write a thoroughly insightful piece about Herbert Marcuse's One-Dimensional Man or Judy Blume's Superfudge.

Work on a Cruise Ship: While old reruns of The Love Boat are pretty rad, I've heard that actually working on a cruise ship is not as fun as it seems. I mean to begin with they're not even full of awesome looking dudes from the 70's with sweet 'staches. I know, what a let down right? The plus side of working on a cruise ship is that you have no chance to spend your money, and your room and board is taken care of, so you can rack up a lot of cash. But there are downsides. One is that you work seven days a week for roughly 12 or more hours a day. Another is that you're contractually obligated to work for multi-month periods. Also, you're sternly discouraged from fraternizing with the guests, so there goes your hopes of scoring with the cuties you're waiting on. And I guess for me, the worst part is that I'd be stuck on a fucking boat! Anyways, there's pluses too, but you've already imagined what those are. If wanna learn more, check out CruiseLinesJobs.com.

Work at a Resort: I think a lot applies here that was mentioned in the bit about cruise ships, except you're not stuck on a boat. Still, this kind of work can be pretty rad, even if it's just seasonal. Wanna be connected to various resort jobs? Then check out CoolWorks.com, ClubMedJobs.com, and ResortJobs.com.

Transitions Abroad: Whether you're looking to go overseas to work, study, volunteer, or just fuck off, TransitionsAbroad.com is your one stop portal to almost everything you need to know. Check it out mate!

Join the Peace Corp: What's that old 60's protest slogan? It's like, "Join the Army: See the World, Meet interesting People, and Kill Them." Well the Peace Corp is exactly the same except you change the last part to say "...and do awesome shit for them". With the Peace Corps, you spend two years of your life in a developing country, helping to build up communities, increase economic viability and generally make them better places. While you're not really making much money per se, you'll be gaining language skills, life experiences, and hopefully have a kick ass time. Plus they do actually pay you a wage that allows you to live in a manner similar to the local community, give you full medical benefits for the duration of your service and up to 18 months after you finish, and they give you $5,000-$7,000 when you finish. All you gotta do is give them two years of your life. Check them out at PeaceCorp.gov.

Join Americorps: It's a lot like the Peace Corp that I just talked about but the main difference is that it happens right here in the good old U-S of A. It's perfect for those who are suspicious of other cultures yet still wanna do something righteous for the less fortunate. Technically the arm of Americorps that you'd be involved in is called VISTA (Volunteers in Service to America), the focus of which is to "serve full-time for a year at a nonprofit organization or local government agency, working to fight illiteracy, improve health services, create businesses, strengthen community groups, and much more". Besides your modest living allowance and health care, the government also gives you roughly $5,000 after your year of service is up. But if I'm not mistaken, I think that money has to go towards college. I'll make you a deal: tell them you're going to BAS University and I'll split the money with you. AmeriCorps.gov

Sign Up for Job Corps: If you're one of those folks who's not so good at things like finishing high school or staying out of jail, but you're still interested in being a productive member of society, I suggest looking into Job Corps. Job Corps is a free education and training program for disadvantaged youth, ages 16-24, who are interested in changing the trajectory of their lives. They not only give you vocational training but also offer to help you get a high school diploma or a GED. Plus once you finish your program they help get employment in the field you trained in. These fields vary from cooking to automotive repair to being a medical assistant. And they even pay you to attend. It's not much at all, but considering they're also paying for your food, housing and education, I guess you can't complain too much. Check out JobCorps.gov if you think you're ready to get your shit together.

Be A Workamper: I don't even know how I stumbled upon this one. So there's this site called Workamper.com which is devoted to finding jobs for people who live out of their RVs. I guess there's a whole culture of people who retire, sell all their shit and then just roll around the country in an RV for the rest of their lives, which actually sounds awesome. But, no one says you have to be a retiree to use this site. If you find yourself wandering the country and looking for some work, link up with the Workamper folks, most of their jobs "are in the Outdoor Hospitality Industry (resorts, campgrounds, theme parks, state/national parks, etc.)".

Be a Guinea Pig: Is there a research hospital in your town? How about a University? If so you can make some decent cash by letting them try stuff out on you. Testing things out on humans is often the final step before they allow something into the market. The plus side of all this is that you'll get paid some cash. The downside is that there is a slight chance you might be infected with some wild shit. It's not likely though considering they've already tried it out on all kinds of monkeys, rabbits and lemurs before it got to you. The best case scenario though happened to Ken Kesey, author of One Flew Over the Cuckoo's Nest. In 1959, the CIA funded a study at the Menlo Park Veteran's Hospital to try out such drugs as lysergic acid diethylamide. Kesey was a volunteer and enjoyed his experiences so much that started bringing some home to give his friends. The name of the drug was shortened to LSD, Kesey and his friends became the Merry Pranksters, and the rest is some strange psychedelic, techno-colored history. I suggest reading Tom Wolfe's The Electric Kool-Aid Acid Test to get the whole story. It's pretty wild.

To find your guinea pig work, check Craigslist under the "ETC" section or contact the university or hospital in area. Just don't mention wanting to experiment with LSD.

Market Research Groups: Market research groups can sometimes pay upwards of $200 or $300 and all you gotta do is hang out for a few hours and answer questions about the things you like. Seriously, sometimes it's as simple as "what kind of vodka do you prefer?". The main place you can find these jobs is under the "ETC" section of Craigslist. Also try bulletin boards in cafes and colleges and the back pages of your local free weekly paper.

Sell Blood and Plasma: Your blood and plasma is not really worth that much. Bummer huh? You thought you were all special because you're this sentient being who can walk around all upright and make and break things with your bare hands, didn't you? You're like, "Oy mate. Dis 'ere blood in me body iz worth many a penny idinit?" Yeah, I speak in a cockney accent when discussing bodily fluids too, but the fact remains that around 30 bucks is what a session of selling blood/plasma will get you. I mean, it ain't too bad considering that they usually give you some cookies and orange juice afterwards, but didn't anyone tell them that's a pretty gross food combination?

If selling your fluids sounds up your alley, just look up where
your nearest blood bank or plasma center is. And if you're feeling
generous you can always donate your juices for free.

Sell your Sperm: We're lucky there were no sperm banks in the
days of William Shakespeare. Could you imagine what twisted stories
that demented bastard would have written? Every other one would've
ended like, "Upon returning from Ye Old Sperm Bank, Mercutio
realized that Rosalyn was his sister (due to his father's sperm
bank donation 20 years prior). He then drowned his son/nephew,
beheaded his wife/sister, and hung himself. The End." Yeah dude...
fuuuuucked up.

Thankfully the chances of unknowingly marrying your sister
are pretty rare, so don't let that keep you from donating your little
swimmers. The thing that should be holding you back is if you're
significantly short, fat, ugly, old, bald, dumb or riddled with disease
because you will most likely be rejected. And being told your man
juice is substandard just isn't something most men want to hear.

Feel like you've got some desirable genes? Then ask your doctor to
recommend a good sperm bank. It might take a while for the sperm
bank to process you, but if you pass their stringent tests, and can
donate fluids a couple times a week for a month or two, you might
be able to pull down a few thousand dollars. For me though, it's
kinda an intellectual Catch 22; if you're tall, smart, good looking, and
disease-free enough to pass their tests, shouldn't you be able to make
money other ways?

Sell Your Eggs: While it's true that the pay scale for professional
men and women is still grossly unequal in the American work force,
all you ladies can at least be proud that you've outshone the fellas in
one lucrative market: baby making. Just one of your eggs is worth
exponentially more than a cup full of sperm. Egg donors can start
off making $7,000 per egg and often times your fee gets upped for
every egg you sell. Unfortunately though it's not an easy process; you
can't just walk into your gynecologist's office, hop in the stirrups and
say, "Doc, I need to pay off some student loans and I saw this pair of
Louboutins that I'm in love with. Think you can pull out a couple
of those puppies for me?". You see love, you yourself are not the egg
bank. If you were, there'd be no such things as gold diggers.

Despite being considered a doctor in Azerbaijan (you'd be surprised how cheaply you can buy an MD there) I'm not allowed to give medical advice here in the States. So if you're serious about selling your eggs, you should talk to your lady parts doctor about it. They can tell you about all the rigorous testing that you'll have to go through, as well as the hormones you'll take, and the surgical procedure that happens at the end of it all. If it all sounds good to you, see if they can hook you up with a donor bank or look for ads on craigslist. Yeah, seriously, you can sell your eggs on Craigslist.

Be a Surrogate Mother: I'm gonna tread lightly here because I've seen this situation lead to a double murder that some how involved Ice-T chasing down some mother who decided not to give up the baby at the very last minute. What, you didn't see that episode of Law & Order: SVU? That show is the shit!

Anyways, you can make a gang of money being a surrogate mother. Seriously, like up to $40,000. The flip side though is that you have to carry a baby for nine months, pop the sucker out, and then give it away. It's real easy to catch feelings about this kind of thing so please think about it long and hard before you decide if the means justify the end.

Sell your Hair: I had a friend in college named Tish who had pretty long hair. Then one day she cut most of it off and donated it to Locks of Love (LocksOfLove.org), a non-profit that gives wigs to underprivileged kids who lose their hair due to chemo. With the hair that she kept, Tish did all kinds of fun things like using green paint to have a permanently rock solid green mohawk. Yeah, I went to UC Santa Cruz where giving stuff to charity and having green mohawks are both considered very cool things. Not everyone is into altruism though, and if you're one of those people who's like, "Fuck the kids, show me the money," then you can always sell those locks of yours.

To have marketable hair, you've got to grow it out, not bleach or dye it, and take care of it...whatever the hell that means. Having long and frumpy hair can be worth it though: you can make some decent cash. At the time I'm writing this, the record amount brought in by someone on BuyandSellHair.com is $3600! Which also reminds me that I didn't tell you about that site yet. If you do wanna grow your mane and sell it, this is the market place where these transactions happen. And yes, it's just as weird as it sounds.

Sell the Stuff You Make: I'm probably the least crafty person on earth; I can't make a damn thing. But I know there's a ton of you who can. While making stuff for your friends and family is all cutesy and shit, might as well try to turn your nimble little fingers into money making machines.

The first thing you can do is try to get involved in local indie craft fairs in your city. These aren't the kind of craft fairs you went to with your mom as a kid, you know the kind with old ladies selling whatever weird crap that old ladies sell. The indie craft fairs I'm talking about usually have bands or djs, alcoholic beverages, and sexy motherfuckers. And what's cool is that these things are popping up all over the country. I'm deeply involved in the SF Indie Mart (Indie-mart.com) and I've been to multiple things like this in Brooklyn too. To find the one nearest you check out IndieCraftShows.com and then get yourself involved. Not only can you sell your swag this way, but you can also network with other like-minded freaks.

If your agoraphobia is acting up and you don't feel like mingling with strangers, never fear, you can always sell your gear online. You can start your own store and sell your crafts on the ever popular Etsy. com. Similarly, you can try IndiePublic.com for all creative things considered "indie". Fancy yourself more of an artist? Hawk your wares at ArtFire.com, "the artisan marketplace home to artists from around the globe".

What if you're not exactly crafty but wanna sell gear with your designs on it? There are magical websites for that too. Check out Zazzle.com or CafePress.com to do exactly what I just said. And if you're making really cool stuff, send some to me. I'll totally wear it.

Sell All Your Media NOW: Let's face it, DVDs and CDs aren't worth a whole lot now that pretty much everything can be downloaded for free. But they are still worth something. Next time you have a day off, rip all your CDs and DVDs to your computer, and then go sell them. You'll still have the songs and movies for when you want to enjoy them, but you'll have the money you collected from selling them as well. The best place to sell them is any used record store. Also, invest in an external hard drive so you can store everything. At the time I'm writing this you can get a 500 gigabyte external for as little as $60 online, and you can pretty much store every digital thing you own on it.

Freelance Manual Labor: Remember in high school when you'd hang outside of a liquor store and try to get cool looking adults to buy some booze for you? Well if you can follow simple directions and are pretty good at not accidentally maiming yourself or others, you can use the same technique to get some work. Just go hang outside of a Home Depot or a hardware store and let the people going in and out know that you're looking for work. Of course it's not a surefire way to get work, but it certainly can happen if you need it too. Personally, I hate manual labor. My hands are for loving and writing, not working and fighting.

Work on a Farm: Once again, manual labor is not my cup of tea. But for those of you who don't mind that kind of thing, you can always go work on a farm. Depending on the job you take, you might only get paid in food and lodging. Other jobs will pay you a decent wage but what you eat and where you sleep will be on your shoulders. Regardless, you'll get to experience all the wonders of back breaking outdoor work. If you're looking for this kinda of work in the southern parts of the US, and aren't a Mexican day laborer, it might be hard to get a gig. Those cats are generally willing to work for less than you are. Consider doing it in Canada, the northern parts of the US or overseas.

There are a lot of different websites out there that can connect you with farms and farmers. You'll have to decide which one is best for you. PickYourOwn.org lists a bunch of farms that are looking for seasonal help and then leaves it up to you to contact them yourself. World Wide Opportunities on Organic Farms (wwoof.org) does the same but only focuses on organic farms. As you can tell by the name, their listings are local and international. PickingJobs.com is also another good site for finding fruit picking jobs all over the world.

Broke-Ass Porn

Once a week at brokeassstuart.com we present Broke-Ass Porn. It's visually stimulating material for the financially impaired. If this shit doesn't get you going, you're not as broke as you thought:

The 10,000 dollar bill

Look at that sexy beast...wow. Could you imagine holding this bill? You'd be like, "Shit, man. I've got $10,000 in my wallet. Fuck buying a bacon wrapped hot dog, I can buy the whole cart and still have change left over to buy all the bootlegged DVDs on Mission Street!!"

There was a time, back before the interwebs, when banks used big bill denominations to transfer money between each other. Instead of sending over tons of bags filled with $100 bills the US Mint printed up these fatty fuckers. There was everything from a $500 bill up to a $100,000 bill.

What's crazy is that these big bills were taken out of circulation back in 1969, which means that old Mr. Chase up there was actually worth about $58,000 last time he was used. Imagine walking around with that in your pocket? I'd feel nervous as shit.

Someone once told me a story that they were in line at the post office and a really old fella turned and showed my friend a $1000 bill that he had in his wallet. To answer your question, no he didn't beat up the old guy and take the money, but just to be safe that old guy should really stop waving around his $1000 bill.

10 Reasons Why Doing Good Stuff for the World Is Actually Good for You and Your Wallet

(I originally wrote this article for Tonic.com, which is a website all about doing good stuff for the world.)

Hey, I'm not saying there's anything wrong with wanting to do good, I'm just saying that there's gotta be a little part of you that's wondering, "What's in this for me?" Right? Come on, you can be honest with Uncle Broke-Ass, I won't tell anyone. Look, whether you admit it or not, I don't really care: I'm just here to show you a few ways that being a goody-two-shoes can actually be beneficial to you AND your scrawny little bank account. They're in no particular order, so don't ask.

1. Feeding the Homeless: This one is a no brainer. Go down to your nearest homeless shelter and ask how you can volunteer. Then do it. After the shift is done you generally get to eat some of the food you've been doling out all day. I know that PB&Js and vegetable soup doesn't sound all that amazing, but after three hours of serving it and not eating it, there is nothing you want more in the world. Plus you got to drink all the coffee you want for free. A homeless shelter without unlimited free coffee is just one big smelly riot waiting to happen.

2. Planting Trees: Who needs a gym membership when you're outside working with a shovel and hoe all day long? Check out the Arbor Day Foundation www.arborday.org for more information about tree planting than you can possibly fathom. And fellas, physical labor isn't just good for the muscles, chicks dig a guy who's a little dirty and smells a bit like man stink. They say there's a lot of pheromones in men's sweat.

3. Recycle: Collecting bottles and cans isn't just for little old bag ladies and homeless Vietnam Vets anymore. You, yes you, can cash in on the craze that's sweeping the nation (well, swept the nation 20 years ago): Recycling! All you gotta do is get a bag (or a shopping cart), pick up the aluminum cans and plastic bottles you see everywhere, and take them to your nearest recycling center (often found near supermarkets in the suburbs). You my friend might be able to make a whole $10!!!

4. Volunteer: Just go volunteer anywhere. Do you know how good that shit looks on your resume or college application? It's like in elementary school when your teacher would put gold stars on your homework, except it's better. It's like a gold star from god or Barack Obama or something.

5. Hang Out with Old People: Old people are often lonely and looking for someone to talk to. That person can be you. Sure they might repeat themselves 15 times, but it's like free entertainment because they've got awesome stories that prove how big of pussies your entire generation is. Plus, if they like you enough, maybe they'll put you in their will.

6. Always Tip 20 Percent: Alright, I really just put this one in here because I've waited tables for most of my adult life. But seriously, being a good tipper is like being a patron of the arts. There's a good chance your waiter is involved in the arts in some way and you tipping well ensures that they won't starve to death or run out of drugs. And also it's just the right thing to do for an extra $1 or $2.

7. Ride a Bike: Not only are you saving Mother Earth from choking to death on exhaust fumes, you're saving yourself a ton of money on car payments, insurance, and gas. It's also a good way to lose some of that Budweiser weight you've been carrying around since junior year of college. And think about how good your legs will look in a skirt or a utility kilt.

8. Get a Reusable Water Bottle: Apparently the number one thing in American landfills is plastic water bottles, so getting a reusable one (like a Nalgene bottle) is like being eco-conscious and accessorizing. Not only can you get different colors to match different outfits, you can finally have a place to put those damn Phish stickers you've been carrying around since tour in '99.

9. Composting: Why pay for shit (literally) to grow your plants in when you can grow them in stuff that's rotting? I'm not sure which actually smells worse, but at least if you grow your veggies in compost you can be all organic man. Check out HowtoCompost.org to learn all about it.

10. Buy My Books: Sure this is shameless self promotion, but seriously if you're into stuff that's cheap and local with healthy amount of shit talking, there's no better resource in the world...except maybe my website (BrokeAssStuart.com).

How much do I love you for buying this book? This much!

mike force

How to Be Broke
The Upside of Being Unemployed

By Ashley Friedman

The worst part of about looking for work is the days in between. You have no idea how long your money is going to have to last, you have no idea when you can expect to work again and you silently curse every tiny expenditure that you made back when you deluded yourself into believing that this was only going to be for a short period of time.

In these dark days of work-searching, it seems like there is nothing to do but scour Craigslist and monster.com until your eyes bleed, sending out cover letter after cover letter with decreasing enthusiasm until you no longer remember where you applied.

But these difficult, unemployed days are the days of your life as well, and you OWE IT TO YOURSELF to make the best of them. Yeah, it's hard to relax and enjoy life when you're not really sure how you're going to be able to pay your rent, but it is critical. Because you

WILL get a job, you WILL have an income and things WILL be okay. Just trust; there's nothing else you can do.

But in the meantime you've gotta live, dammit, LIVE! Here are some ways to do that.

NAP

It sounds indulgent, I know especially since America equates relaxing with lazy sluggishness, but all people with jobs do is talk about how tired they are all the time. You have no excuse now not to catch up on all the sleep debt you have accrued over the past 20-something years of your life. Lay in bed and read, watch something on hulu and then let yourself drift off for a couple of hours. Remember: every hour you spend asleep is an hour you're not spending money.

BONUS: Sleeping burns more calories than just sitting in front of the TV. Hey, Ladeeeez!

COOK

The Food Network and the Internet are rife with saliva-inducing food imagery, most of which is horrifically unhealthy, or at least prohibitively expensive to make. But there are many websites dedicated to delicious food that is easily made with what you probably already have in your house. Use your abundance of free time to perfect a cookie recipe, try something you've never made before or just simply make a pact to make every single meal at home for a week and see how much cash that saves you. Try 101CookBooks. com, TheAmateurGourmet.com, or www.eatmedelicious.com for baking. Also, check out page 20 for other great cooking websites.

READ

I heard a (mildly funny) standup comic talk about prison recently. "If it weren't for the ass rape," he asserted, "I'd go right now. What do you do in prison beside sleep, work out and read books? It's what you should be doing anyway." No one has time to read anymore and when you're done with your soul-sucking job there's not much else that appeals other than drinking at happy hour or zoning out in front of the TV. The unemployed have the unique opportunity to better themselves, intellectually speaking, and escape into a novel for a few hours a day while everyone else is at work. And there's no financial element at all: a library card in any city is beautifully free, and having to visit the library to get it will give you something else to do.

Not sure what to read? Check out the ModernLibrary.com's 100 Greatest Novels. Sure it skews a bit to the white male side of things but it's important to know one's enemy right? For a bit of a more diverse take on things check out The Guardian's List at www.guardian.co.uk/books/bestbooks. There's also Goodreads.com, which lets you see what people you know are reading and search books, etc. It's like Facebook for nerdy people!

GO OUTSIDE

Really. I know it's hot, I know. But soon it will be cold and it's a lot less easy to have a sense of humor about poverty in the dead of winter, so take advantage.

SEXIN'

This is clearly a no brainer, but it never hurts to reinforce! Its great exercise, very much fun, and unless you're Eliot Spitzer (zing!), it's all marvelously free. When you get a job your brain is going to be all clogged with thought about TPS reports, and casual Friday but for now you have all the time in the world to turn your apartment into a cozy lair of sexual seduction for your partner. Get on it!

GET CREATIVE

If you're a crafty type, you are probably already doing this and have turned several old GWAR t-shirts into tea cozies in the time it has taken you to read this post. If you're Naughty, rather than Crafty by nature (HA!) this is a bit of a harder sell, but believe me, nothing can equal the sense of accomplishment you feel after making something with your own two hands. For project ideas check out CraftyNest.com, the DIY section at DesignSponge.com, or IkeaHacker.com, to change some of your yawn-inducing furniture into crazy original shit!

LAST RESORT: DEEP CLEAN YOUR HOUSE

There is much that is satisfying and very little that is fun about cleaning your house. That said, it's free, people, and it really should be done anyway. This sounds a little OCD and cultish, but in a sense, cleaning a space means taking control of it and that does affect your mindset. Own that bathtub, clean out your refrigerator, and splurge on a new box of baking soda; you deserve it!

After you've scrubbed, scoured, rinsed, and washed, and every surface of your apartment smells lemony fresh, that gleam of accomplishment will shine brightly in your eye. And then you will know that you can, and will, handle any thing this universe chucks at you.

This picture pretty much guarantees that I can never run for public office

Entertainment

Being a broke-ass is about having a great time no matter how little money you have. And while I'm sure you've mastered many different ways of entertaining yourself throughout your years of brokeitude, I figured I'd hip you to some ideas you may not have considered yet. I mean that is why you bought, borrowed or "borrowed" this book isn't it?

Free Tours of Your Town

Yeah I know, you live there and don't need some strange motherfucker leading you around and telling you shit about your city but seriously, this can be a really fun and informative thing to do. Check in with the local tourism board in your area to see what kind of free tours are going on. These tours are often led by local volunteers who have a plethora of knowledge about the places they're showing you. I can totally see myself being one of these people when I'm an old fart.

Sign Up for Email Lists

These days Camper English is an authority on all things booze related. He's contributed to the *San Francisco Chronicle, The Wall Street Journal,* and theAtlanic.com, just to name a few. But at one point he was a shot of Old Crow with a PBR chaser kind of cat, just like you. Back then he wrote a book called *Party Like a Rock Star Even When You're Poor as Dirt.* Even though he's moved on to classier subject matter since *Rock Star,* he still had some pretty great ideas. My favorite has to do with email lists.

 The best way to be in the know about all the cheap and free events going on in your town is to sign up for pretty much every email list you can. I'm talking bands, publicists, event websites (like Flavorpill, Urban Daddy, and Daily Candy), alternative weekly newspapers, clubs, club promoters, clothing stores, museums, restaurants, bars, theatres, and even fucking gyms*. Literally, all that you come across. Now I know you're like, "Motherfucker, I already get enough junk emails telling me shit like I need penis enhancement, and I'm a chick! The last thing I need is more crap to sift through!" and my man Camper has the perfect solution for that: start a new email account that is solely used for email lists. That way every time you're looking for something going on, all you gotta do is log into that account and skim over the emails that are sitting there. If you do this, you will always be one of the first to hear about pretty much everything, including all the deals, specials and giveaways that are being done. Genius, right? Dude should have stayed in the broke game huh? Well at least he didn't sell out and become a land developer or some shit. Holding it down as an authority on booze is pretty much what we're all aspiring to do anyways.

Pay What You Can Nights

Many theaters and museums have at least one night a week or month where you can pay only as much as you wish to give. At theaters, these are often at the beginning of a run or during the final dress rehearsal. For museums, usually on a Friday night during extended hours, which–warning–will be super crowded with art-hungry

---

Since we're discussing it, don't forget to go to BrokeAssStuart.com and sign up for my email list. It will totally make you sexier.

cheapsters just like you so wear your patience pants (I go into this more in the dating section on page 151). Museums post these on its website and for theater, just drop by or call some theaters to see when they have a Pay What You Can Night to get your high brow on.

Get a Student ID

Who cares if you're not a student anymore? You still want student discounts right? While the days are over when you could just walk down the street in New York's East Village and be offered to have a fake ID made for you (this happened to me when I was 16), you can still get a real student ID at STA Travel. Just go in there and inquire about a packaged trip and before you go, tell them that you've got to think about it but that you'll be back. If at that point they don't try to sell you an international student ID, just ask if you can get one. Most of the time they never bother to check if you're actually a student. And when you have it, use it by asking EVERYONE if they have student discounts. Sometimes even if they don't, they'll feel like they should and give you one anyways.

Volunteer Ushering

Want to see a great show for free? Volunteer to be an usher. Many theatres and music venues would rather have someone do it for free than pay someone to usher, so if there's a show you're interested in seeing, contact the venue it's playing at to inquire about ushering. Truth be told, you've gotta get on it as soon as you hear about a show. There's only a limited number of spots and tons of people want them. The more often you do it, assuming you do a good job, the more likely they are to give you extra consideration for each gig.

Rec Centers

Go play a pick up game of basketball or badminton at your neighborhood Rec Center or playground. Do pick up games of badminton even exist? I guess if you try it, report back and let me know. Just pick a sport you actually know how to play so people will invite you back.

Alternative Reality Games

So there's this thing in San Francisco called The Jejune Institute and it's two of the best hours I've ever spent in my life. From the moment you arrive on the 16th floor of 580 California Street and tell the receptionist that you're there for the Jejune Institute, you've done the equivalent of taking the red pill from *The Matrix*. The receptionist hands you a key with directions to a certain room in the office, and every step you take afterwards is completely mind-blowing. I don't want to give anything away, but what you embark on is an exploration of San Francisco in ways you never imagined possible. It's like being on the show Lost but instead of dodging weird fucking smoke monsters and "the Others", you're gallivanting around the city unlocking different clues. Every part of the puzzle opens up other things to be discovered.

While the Jejune Institute at first seems like some kind of new age cult, it's really something called an Alternative Reality Game (ARG). The modern day oracle known as Wikipedia defines ARGs as:

An alternate reality game (ARG) is an interactive narrative that uses the real world as a platform, often involving multiple media and game elements, to tell a story that may be affected by participants' ideas or actions. The form is defined by intense player involvement with a story that takes place in real-time and evolves according to participants' responses, and characters that are actively controlled by the game's designers, as opposed to being controlled by artificial intelligence as in a computer or console video game. Players interact directly with characters in the game, solve plot-based challenges and puzzles, and often work together with a community to analyze the story and coordinate real-life and online activities. ARGs generally use multimedia, such as telephones, email and mail but rely on the Internet as the central binding medium.

Basically what it's saying is that ARGs are fucking awesome. They're completely immersive games where you may never know who is in charge and the next clue you get might be from a random stranger on the street, a text message, or an email. And it's not all creepy like that Michael Douglas movie *The Game*, it's just a lot of fun. Does this sound like something you wanna get in on? If so check out argn.com to see what games are currently happening and how you can participate. And seriously if you are in or around San Francisco, you have to do the JeJune Institute.

Geocaching

According to GeoCaching.com: "Geocaching is a high-tech treasure hunting game played throughout the world by adventure seekers equipped with GPS devices. The basic idea is to locate hidden containers, called geocaches, outdoors and then share your experiences online. Geocaching is enjoyed by people from all age groups, with a strong sense of community and support for the environment." I haven't done it myself but I've got friends that are hooked. Find a GPS device (there's probably an app for that at this point) and get moving on that shit. There's over a million active geocache sites around the world. It's probably wise to explain to friends what you're looking for before you start pawing through that pile of leaves though.

Watch a Trial

If you're really bored, you can always go down to the courthouse and watch a trial. I'm sure a lot of them are super boring but maybe if you're lucky you'll get to see some interesting Jeffery Dahmer-type shit. At the very least you can entertain yourself by saying BUM BUM (the sound from *Law & Order*) between each part of the trial. As you can tell, I wasn't kidding when I said I was obsessed with *Law & Order*.

Free Internet Access

As you probably know, there's free wi-fi all over the world. There's millions of places where you can just open your laptop, log on and voila!– you're ready to post a missed connection about that sexy redhead you just saw on the train. But sometimes it can be hard to find a place that has it. Luckily there's a website called WiFiFreeSpot.com that tells you all the different places to find some free signals. It covers places in the US, Europe and other parts of the world. I'm a big fan of the Internet. It's pretty amazing that we live in an age where the answer to 99% of your questions can just be obtained through google.

Seeing Movies

Seeing movies is great and all but it can be pretty expensive. I mean in cities like San Francisco and New York, movies cost over

$10! That's just ridiculous. What follows is a list of ways you can see all kinds of movies without having to come out of pocket.

Beanbag Chairs and Popcorn: Why pay $10 to see a movie when you can see one for free? Student Unions at Universities are generally charged with finding things to do for the boring kids who don't wanna go out and party. This often involves sitting on beanbag chairs and watching free movies. Inquire at the Student Union for screening details. Other university free movie options include attending film department screenings and even using the screening room at the campus library (also a convenient make-out room).

Buy Children's Tickets: No I don't mean search out random children to buy tickets for you, you fucking weirdo. Julia Wertz, author/illustrator of Fart Party (FartParty.org) made this great suggestion when she was Broke-Ass of the week on my site. I asked her what her best money saving tip was and she responded: "buying movie tickets from the kiosk and getting a child or senior ticket for $4 less. They usually never notice and if they do, play dumb and they'll usually let you go. I only got caught once and all I had to do was go get a refund and pay for an adult ticket." Well played, Julia, well played.

Second Run Movie Houses and Midnight Matinees: Every town has a theatre that plays old movies for less than half the price of a regular ticket. Whether it's a movie that was just in theatres six months ago, or the annual 4/20 showing of The *Big Lebowski*, second run theatres are the shit. Some of them are even as cheap as $1 like at Movies 10 in Rochester, NY. Sure you may not have been able to take part in the water cooler conversation about some super awesome action movie when it came out, but honestly who the fuck hangs out around a water cooler anyways? What the hell kind of *Dilbert* life do those people live?

Midnight matinees are also great ways to see movies for cheaper than regular price. These usually happen on Fridays and Saturday nights and they mostly play second run and old films. Plus it makes for a great night out if you're trying to stay off the hooch. Just ask your sponsor. Then again, I also know people who bring a bottle when they go to midnight matinees. If you're trying to stay sober, don't sit by anyone who looks like me.

Bar Movie Nights: Speaking of drinking at the movies, lots of bars do movie nights towards the beginning of the week. Not only is it a great chance to watch *Dazed and Confused* or *Point Break* for the 17th time, it's also an occasion to get some cheap booze. Bars that do movie nights usually have drink specials to accompany them. Win-win!

Movie Hopping: I'm sure most of you have done this before, but for that small percentage of you who hasn't, all I gotta say is: Buck up! What are you afraid of, getting arrested? That's not gonna happen, the worst that will go down is that they will kick you out of the movie theater and tell you not to come back. But come on, it's not likely that their even gonna remember what you look like.

But anyways, for those of you who don't know what movie hopping is, it's when you pay to see one movie but then see multiple ones that day. In fact, if you really don't have shit to do you can make a full day of it. Pack a lunch and some beer or a flask and hit up a matinee. Then when your movie is over, just walk out with the throng of people and make your way into the next one you want to see. The best way to go about it is to make a little game plan ahead of time. Figure out which movies you want to see that day, and bring a listing of their times with you (either print it out from the computer or get it from the newspaper). Then when you first get to the cinema, scout out which movies are in which theatres. That way you'll know exactly where to go when it's time to see the next movie. And the most important part of all of this is to just act normal. If you look like you're trying to be sneaky, they will think something is up.

Guerrilla Drive-In Movies: Most old school drive-ins are used for swap meets these days. What can you do? I mean, it's usually technology that drives a culture forward and because of this, outdated things (no matter how cool they are) often get left behind. But the people involved with MobMov.org are trying to change that. Short for Mobile Movie, MobMov is, "the global guerilla drive-in movement bringing back the forgotten joy of the great American drive-in. Thanks to the wonders of modern technology, what used to be a dark and decrepit warehouse wall springs to life with the sublime sights and sounds of a big-screen movie. Best of all, the MobMov is free." People drive up to an abandoned warehouse or other big unused wall, tune their radios to the frequency playing the movie sound, and then sit back and enjoy a motion picture. There are hundreds of chapters across the globe, so just go to the website to see which one is closest to you.

Rooftop and Park Movies: What could be better than going to a rooftop or a park with cheap wine and cheap friends, and watching classic movies with hundreds of other revelers? Nothing. Every time I've gone to something like this it always ended up being a great night. They usually happen in the summertime. Google the name of your town and "rooftop movies" or "park movies" to find out what's cracking in your part of the world.

Get Free Movie Tickets: A lot of times theaters will run promotional screenings of movies that are about to come out. They do this to help create word of mouth buzz; they want you go out and tell all your little friends how awesome such and such movie was. They figure you got a big mouth. You probably do. So how do you get your paws on tickets to such free screenings? The internet, that's how.

A good place to start is FilmMetro.com. The way it works is, you sign up for a free membership and then enter your city and state. Then you find out which screenings are around you and you click on the one you want. Then you simply reserve your tickets and print them. While the tickets go quickly, the site lets you know what day they're gonna be available. Then on that day, it gives you and hour/minute countdown, so you've just gotta be ready to swoop them then. Another site that lets you get free movie passes is Wild About Movies. If you go to WildAboutMovies.com/screenings you can print passes to tons of different flicks. All you gotta do is scroll to the bottom and click on your city. Then find the movie you wanna see click on it, click on the thing that says, "Print Passes to _____" and follow directions. Actually, fuck it, why am I even walking your though this shit step by step? If you can't figure this out by yourself, you're hopeless. Just note that while Wild About Movies looks like it's just full of spam (it kinda is) you can still actually get movie tickets from it. Another such website is GoFoBo.com except this one looks a lot less sketchy.

Stream Movies for Free: If you don't want to go through all the hassle of trying to wrangle free tickets, or you don't feel like actually going to a movie theater or doing the whole Netflix thing, you can always just stream a movie. There are literally scores of sites out there that let you pick almost any movie you want and watch it on your computer for free. Just to name a few: solarmovie.com, movies-links.tv, missedashow.net, tvshack.net...really the list goes on for a long time. Some of these have higher production quality than others. One such is Hulu.com but all the studios are involved with Hulu and control what they offer, so you'll likely find yourself watching a movie that you would never watch if you had to pay for it. If you're in the mood for foreign or independent films, Auteurs.com is an awesome membership-based site that offers free movies and also some at cost.

How to **Lower your Cable Bill**

The cable companies always sucker you in by giving you some amazing introductory rate, and then hiking it up six months to a year after you join. It's one of those things that you forget about until one day you look at your bill and say, "What the fuck? Why did this double?" and then you look to make sure your dirtbag roommate didn't order late night porno channels when he came home wasted. He probably did.

Well, just last week I was appalled at what we were paying for cable so I called the cable company up. I did some research beforehand to see what kind of sweet introductory rates they were offering at the time, and I asked to be switched to one of those. Unfortunately they said no, but then I said, "You know, I've been thinking of switching to the Dish Network because they are offering me a better deal, but I'm really happy with the service you're giving me. Is there any way you can lower my rate?" At that point they switched me to some kind of "Retention Department" and the lady there was able to take almost $40 off my bill! Not too shabby huh? These companies obviously want to keep you (and your money) so they can be more flexible than you think. Plus I think you would get the same result if you have Dish Network and threaten them that you are thinking of moving to cable.

So there you have it. Give it a try and drop me an email to let me know how it goes.

Concerts

The Old Hand Stamp Trick: If you've got any true old-school style hippie friends you know the only thing they hate more than war and sobriety is paying to get into shows. The first year the Outside Lands Festival happened in SF one of my hippie friends said to me, "There is no way those fences can keep me out." And he was right. He totally got in for free.

I went to college at UC Santa Cruz, a place where Growing Dreads for White People 101 could have been a very well-attended class had it been offered. Because of this I've met many hippies in my day and some of them have let me in on some of their secret concert magic.

Some of them said, "Look, Stu, if you just, you know, hang out in front of the venue with your finger pointing to the sky and occasionally tell passersby 'look bro I need a miracle' you're bound to get a ticket somehow." The problem with these cats is that they often enjoyed being outside the concert with the rest of the slackers almost more than actually seeing the show. The main trick I learned from my Tom's Deodorant-wearing brethren was the old hand stamp trick. There are many ways to go about it, but the basic premise is one person pays, goes in, gets their hand stamped, comes back out to "smoke a cigarette", and then transfers the image of their stamp on to the hands of other people.

One way to do it is to lick the original stamp (or moisten it another way if you're a germaphobe), and then press it onto someone else's hand. This only works though if there are no words, if there are, they will show up backwards. Another way to do it is to have a friend who's good at drawing and has a few sharpies. Choose the color that matches the ink and then have them trace the original, then press it on the new hand. If they're real good they can freehand draw it. Then all of you can go back in and enjoy the show. For future reference, never ask me to draw anything freehand. I will most certainly disappoint you.

Get There Early: If you're going to a DJ night or even some local live music at a small club you can always avoid paying the cover by showing up before they charge it. When I used to throw shows I always hated these fuckers because I knew they were gaming me. But since I'm a way better at being a broke-ass than I was a concert promoter, I gotta give those cats props. The reason this works is because, generally speaking, all the money from the door goes to the promoter, not the bar. The bar makes its money on booze. Therefore if you show up 10 or 20 minutes before things get popping, the bar is still gonna let you in because it wants your booze money.

Lend a Helping Hand: There's almost no such thing as overnight success. Almost everyone who's ever made it big has done so by standing on the shoulders of those willing to help out. If you really like a local band, volunteer to be part of their street team. This means handing out flyers, putting up posters and spreading the word. At this point I'm too old and cranky to care this much about a band, but when I was younger and still believed in things, this was a good way to be involved. Not only did it feel like I was part of something, it usually netted me free CDs* and entrance to shows.

But let's say the bands you want to see are too big to need help from you. Just find out if any of the radio stations are involved in promoting the show. If they are contact them and inquire about volunteering to be on the street team in exchange for some tickets.

This also goes for big festivals as well. Find out what venders are going to be working the show and see if they will hire you on to work. While they may or may not pay you, you'll certainly get free entrance to the festival and probably only have to work a minimal amount of hours.

Join the Fan Club: No, I don't mean the stalker club that hangs out and tries to fuck the band (though that's probably the easiest way to get free tickets, and many other things that might not be as desirable and burn a little). By "joining the fan club" I mean just that; sign up for whatever list they've got going on. You'll be the first to know about any secret shows they're doing or any ticket discount codes they send out.

Music Blogs: These can often be completely inane and annoying to read, but many music blogs do ticket giveaways. Shit, my site isn't even focused on music and I still do giveaways. Stay up on various music sites and enter to win free shit. You'd be surprised what you can win. I

You must remember this was before all media was "free." CDs used to actually cost money.

actually just won a six-month supply of Vitamin Water from a contest I didn't even know I was entered in. I must admit, the novelty of having that much VW has certainly worn off and now I'm overwhelmed by the sheer amount of it sitting in my living room. Well that, and its wondrous body replenishing electrolytes too of course*.

In-Store Concerts: At the time I'm writing this, the future of music stores is kinda hanging by a thread. While there will most likely always be record stores of some kind, many of the larger stores that previously supported big name in-store concerts are falling to the wayside. That being said other types of stores are starting to slip in and fill that void. Many Apple stores now do in-store concerts as do some of the big name bookstores like Barnes & Noble; even better, check out your local independent record store to see if they do, too. Wouldn't it be amazing if the indie stores rose from the rubble of the fallen corporation giants and made money again? And if you're ever in Berkeley, San Francisco, or Hollywood, try to catch one of Amoeba's epic in-stores.

Seeing Art

Museums: I cover this in far more depth over in the dating section of this book (see page 151), but as a quick note, most museums have a day where it's either free or "pay what you can". So go forth and expand your mind, or as the great luminary George Clinton once said, "Free your mind and your ass will follow." Yeah, I guess that's not really related to this at all.

Art Openings: Every town has art galleries and every gallery has art openings. In most cities there's generally one day at the beginning of the month where a huge portion of the galleries do their openings. For example, in San Francisco it's the first Thursday of the month. Art openings are brilliant for broke-asses because they generally mean two things, free wine and free cheese. Being, well…being me, I simply can't resist a place that will let me eat and drink for free while looking at pretty girls and neat shit on the walls. The only problem with art openings is that a lot of art seems like utter crap. I know you

---

*Vitamin Water, please make out that check to Stuart Schuffman. Thanks!

know what I'm talking about. Don't give me that, "It's all perspective" bullshit, we both know there's a lot of crap out there masquerading as art. But it's totally worth getting your eyeballs abused by bad art in exchange for free wine, cheese, and the potential to meet hotties right? I thought so. Find out when the openings are in your town.

Open Studios: Open Studios happens a few times a year and is basically when tons of artists open up their studios (surprise!) and let people come through and check out their stuff. If you live somewhere near a university, Open Studios generally happens at the end of each quarter or semester. Otherwise just Google "open studios" and the name of your town. Often times it can be a big event and ends up being a party-like atmosphere. Free wine and cheese abounds, so might drinking too much of said wine and accidentally puncturing a hole in someone's painting, but at least you got to meet some cool people living in your neighborhood.

Reading

Get a Library Card: Not only can you borrow millions of great books for spending one minute to get a free card, but you can also borrow CDs, DVDs and other media too. Plus, you can even go online to request what you want without even stepping foot out your door, and when it's ready they hold for you in a special area so you can get swiftly in and out for that copy of MacGruber without anyone seeing.

Better World Books: Sure Amazon has just about every book in the world at ridiculously low prices, but what do they do that's good for the world? Assuming you haven't been gifted (or even bought) and iPad or a Kindle yet, you probably read books the old fashioned way: holding them. If that's the case, and you buy your books online, don't buy them from Amazon. Buy them from BetterWorldBooks. com. To quote the website, "Better World Books is a for-profit social enterprise, that collects used books and sells them online to raise money for literary initiatives worldwide." All the new and used books are sold cheaply and if you're in the US there's no shipping fees (they only charge $3.97 worldwide anyways). Plus by buying used books, you're saving them from ending up in landfills. What's better than doing good for the world while buying a book?

Library Book Sales: Even libraries gotta sell their shit sometimes to help pay the bills. When they do this it gives you a chance to swoop in on some books for super cheap. Books often cost only 50 cents to a dollar at these sales and they happen yearly. The library totally appreciates your help, as do the moms and dads who use the DVD collection to keep their kids entertained and quiet on the weekends.

Great Novels About Being Broke

Almost all of us have figured out a way to legitimize our brokenness to ourselves. Whether you're an aspiring artist, a starving student, an underpaid idealist, just got laid off, or simply can't hold down a regular job, you've found a way to explain to yourself (and everyone else) why you are where you are. That's why I put together the following list of the best novels about being broke. Sure some of them romanticize brokeitude as something bohemian, but hell, Jack London said it best when he mused, "You look back and see how hard you worked and how poor you were, and how desperately anxious you were to succeed, and all you can remember is how happy you were."

Some of these aren't romantic at all, they're just good books about really poor people. Regardless, if you're broke there's no better way of entertaining yourself than reading a book; you can borrow all of these for free from the library. Note: This list is by no way complete, so don't get your panties in a bunch if I've left something out.

The Adventures of Oliver Twist by Charles Dickens
(published in serial from 1837-1839)
This book single handedly made it ok for grubby little orphans to express themselves through song and dance. Or was that the movie? Either way, I personally think Dickens writes like an asshole, but invite you to judge for yourself by reading his complete works for free at Dickens-Literature.com.

Hunger by Knut Hamsun (1890)
The original starving artist novel, *Hunger* is all about, well, starving artistically. The main character wanders around obsessing about food, while slowly losing his mind. He refuses to take on a

regular job and would rather starve than earn money not creating
art. Basically imagine what Williamsburg, Silver Lake, The Mission,
or any other hipster neighborhood would be like if those peoples'
parents' weren't paying their bills. It's a frightening thought.
Down and Out in Paris and London by George Orwell (1933)
   George Orwell flirts with bohemian life while washing dishes in
Paris and tramping around London. He doesn't let on about this
too much, but despite being an "artist," his parents float him money
when he needs it. This sets an obvious precedent. Luckily, if you're
too lazy to go to the library you can always read George Orwell's
complete work for free at George-Orwell.org.

Tropic of Cancer by Henry Miller (1934)

Ditching his wife in Brooklyn, Henry Miller lands himself in Paris
and lives off other people's kindness…yeah, he becomes a bum, errrr,
uh, a struggling writer. Considered groundbreaking for its use of
stream of consciousness writing (which I actually find quite annoying
in this case) *Tropic of Cancer* is also considered revolutionary for its
graphic and visceral descriptions of sex. It wasn't even allowed to be
published in the US until 1961. This book pretty much paved the way
for all the foul-mouthed and dirty-minded writers who've come since.
Big ups to Henry!

The Grapes of Wrath by John Steinbeck (1938)

As its name suggests, The Great Depression was really, really
depressing. This book is about life during that time and so candid that
only thing even remotely worth romanticizing in this book is when a
starving man gets breast fed, and even that feels kind of wrong.

Ask the Dust by John Fante (1939)

Probably John Fante's most successful book (and by successful, I
mean not very), *Ask the Dust* is about a young Italian-American,
Arturo Bandini, who moves to LA during the Depression to be a
writer. He of course struggles with his art, then meets a hot Mexican
girl, and a series of bad things happen. Charles Bukowski considered
Fante to be one of his favorite writers.

On the Road by Jack Kerouac (1957)

Jack meets Neal. Much hitchhiking, drinking, latent homoeroticism,

Benzedrine, and hanky-panky occurs. Jack writes *On the Road* and includes the most famous Roman Candle metaphor ever. Bohemians are redefined as anyone who realizes that the only people for them are "the mad ones."

Angela's Ashes by Frank McCourt (1996)

Nothing romantic about this one; Frank McCourt's childhood was fuuuuucked up! Personally, I had a great time in Limerick, Ireland (where the book takes place) and ended up partying all night long with some local bartenders, and didn't even get knifed despite the town's nickname of "Stab City." McCourt unfortunately did not have close to the great of time in Limerick as I did, but his story is way more important.

Dishwasher by Pete Jordan (2007)

Well-loved 'zinester, Dishwasher Pete traveled around the country trying to wash dishes in all 50 states. This book tells his story and details all the strange and wonderful things that go along with being the world's most famous dishwasher. Dishwasher Pete also gives props to all his dish dog predecessors including George Orwell.

Anything ever written by Charles Bukowski

The patron saint of all broke-asses, outsiders, and losers, Bukowski wrote about life in starkly real terms through themes like sex, alcohol, prostitution, horse races, bar fights, and loneliness. Most of all, he wrote about Los Angeles. Despite being well known for his poetry and short stories, he also wrote six novels in his lifetime: *Post Office* (1971), *Factotum* (1975), *Women* (1978), *Ham on Rye* (1982), *Hollywood* (1989) and Pulp (1994). *Women* is my personal favorite and a good place to start if you've never read his work before.

How to Get Free Concert Tickets for "Members of the Press"

By Andrew Dalton (Dolfapedia.org)

Let me get something straight, I kind of hate music writers. I mean I like to hear about what people like, but the fluffy descriptions of some new band's prominent use of a Playskool tape recorder on their latest record do nothing to tell me about the band's sound. And the endless comparisons to earlier bands that I've never heard of feel like underhanded attempts by the writer to give me an inferiority complex. So the natural thing to do is to set out on your own! Start that music blog that you write in your head every time you listen to a new record. Write down what you would tell your friend if he asked you what you thought of a new band or album or song or whatever. It doesn't even have to be the newest or the hippest, just write about what you like or you'll find yourself trying too hard and there are already a ton of bloggers out there who beat you too it. Remember: the goal here is free tickets, not an immensely popular website (although that would be nice).

The next step, once you've got like...I dunno three posts or so up on your site (which probably still has the default theme for your blogging platform of choice) is to start emailing PR reps. PR reps for small-to-mid-level bands are some of the friendliest people on the Internet. And by friendliest, I mean they'll never stop sending you emails once you get on their mailing list. This is OK if you're a bit obsessive about music anyway because oftentimes you'll find out about bands that are coming to town before the venues even announce it. On the flipside, PR reps love to sound super excited about every band they represent even if you think the band is total crap, so you'll have to do some filtering to find the good stuff.

Once you see a show announcement for a band you like, start emailing them back. Ask nicely for a press pass to a show and tell them you'd like to "provide some coverage" or "hype up this band" or drop some other buzzwords that make you sound like you know what you're doing. I'm 99% sure most (surely not all) PR reps don't actually read the sites that request press passes to events and they certainly don't have the time to go looking up how much traffic you get so they won't notice if you're mom and your old college roommate are the only people reading the site. Also, it's always a good idea to request a +1 so you don't have to go to the show alone. Or you can disguise this by requesting a Photo Pass and bringing your friend who is a "photographer" along. (Borrow someone's fancy DSLR for added authenticity.)

And that's pretty much it! You're already on the list so go enjoy the show. Although it is a good idea to actually write a review or even just a wrap-up of your impressions from the show in the days after. Send a link for your review along to the PR rep who put you on the list so they'll start to think you're legit. And if nothing else at least you can use the "I'm a music blogger" line to pick up members of the opposite sex.

Note from Broke-Ass Stuart: this kind of thing has also worked for me for movie passes, free dinners, and free drinks. Plus publicists and labels will also send you free music.

Broke-Ass Porn

Once a week at brokeassstuart.com we present Broke-Ass Porn. It's visually stimulating material for the financially impaired. If this shit doesn't get you going, you're not as broke as you thought:

Park Days

The sun is out. (Or at least imagine it is.) Birds are chirping, tan lines are appearing, and the sound of laughter and acoustic guitars can be heard coming from any city park. What more can you ask for in life than to be able to hang out with friends (ones you've just met or the ones you've known for years), while enjoying the warm sun and some cold beers? It's a broke-ass's dream, really. The atmosphere is free and the only thing you have to pay for is whatever you decide to bring.

Some of the best days of my life have been spent in parks, from Dolores in SF to Prospect in BK; from the Tiergarten in Berlin to that weird time in Argentina with the Native American and the Norwegian cokeheads. I love hanging in the park because it's one of the few places you can go where the amount of enjoyment you get has absolutely no correlation to the amount of money in your pocket. Even the bums seem to have a great time on a nice day in the park.

So next time the sun is shining and you've got some free time on your hands, grab a blanket, a tall boy, and some pals, and head to the park. It's beckoning you, but you already knew that. Just remember one thing, don't be an inconsiderate shithead. Make sure to pick up your trash when you leave... you're a grown person for fuck's sake!

Apparently after a certain amount of drinks I turn into Hunter S. Thompson

Drinking

If you couldn't tell by now, I like to drink. What can I say? I'm a creature of the night, and a very thirsty one at that. But that shit can get hella expensive. Which is why you should read this chapter. It'll make you a better alcoholic. Wait, that's not a good thing is it?

Buybacks: A buyback is when, after you buy a few rounds, the bartender buys the next one. While it doesn't always happen, if it does, it's after the third or fourth round. Luckily, there are a few things you can do to help make sure you get one. Here's some tips:

1. Try to order from the same bartender all night long.
2. Tip extra well on the first drink and at least a buck a drink after that.
3. If it's not too busy try to chat a little with the barkeep, or at least say your pleases and thank yous.

4. Keep your orders simple and try to order the same things all night long.

5. Offer to buy the bartender a drink. Even if they accept, they probably won't charge you.

If you do all these things, you are almost guaranteed to win the bartender's favor and at least one free drink. If it doesn't happen, this usually means one of three things:

1. The bar has super strict pouring rules. You probably shouldn't have been drinking there in the first place.

2. The bartender is as dick. Try not to give him/her your business again.

3. The bartender remembers last time you were there and you got 86'd for whatever the hell it was you got 86'd for.

Buy the Bartender a Shot: Outside of a recent event in Los Angeles, every I time I offer to buy the bartender a shot they never actually charge me for it. But since they think I'm legit for offering, they end up taking good care of me for the rest of the night. This usually means giving me a free drink or two or not making me wait too long before I'm served. And in a few lovely instances it led to them taking care of me for the night in a far naughtier way.

Industry Professional Courtesy: Service industry people take care of each other and always try to hook each other up. It's because they all know they have to deal with the same ridiculous bullshit. So I you go to a bar and say something like, "yeah, I just got off a hellish shift at the restaurant around the corner" chances are the barkeep will buy you a drink. If you are bought a drink, you better tip big because otherwise that bartender will never hook you up again.

Get it on the Rocks: If you're drinking straight liquor, order it on the rocks instead of neat. Because rocks glasses are bigger than shot classes, bartenders usually end up pouring more into them. This way you get more for your money.

Buy a Flask: It's the eternal dilemma: your friends call you an alcoholic if you drink by yourself, but you can't afford to drink at a bar. So what do you do? That's easy! Bring your own booze to the bar. Why else would god have invented flasks? Now all you need to do is pony up the cash for a mixer and pour your own drink on the sly. Just don't get caught or they might not let you come back…ever.

As for the cost of the flask if you wanna be fancy about your drinking you can get a billion different flask variations. But since I know you're not worried about how people perceive you (you're sneaking a flask into a bar for fuck's sake), you can always just get a plastic flask for between $5 and $10. This way you can also get by any metal detectors. Nips (the little airport-sized bottles) sell for $1-$2 and are a quick solution, too.

Or, Make Your Own Flask: Fuck the fancy shit, go to the store and buy yourself a half pint of some cheap booze. When you're done drinking it, peel off the label and use some lighter fluid or nail polish remover to get rid of the sticky residue. Then decorate the thing with some Broke-Ass Stuart stickers (well, you totally should), and boom! You have a new flask.

Industry Night: Landing somewhere between Sunday and Tuesday, Industry Night is when bars lower their prices in order to attract a service industry crowd. This benefits everyone: service industry people often have those nights off and want to go out. Those same nights are generally slow for most bars. As you can see it's a match made in some kind of Dionysian heaven. So while you may not be an industry person yourself, you can certainly still go out and drink on industry nights. Ask around and find out which bars do it. Plus it's a great way to meet servers and bartenders, people who may be inclined to hook you up some how at their place of employment. The tricky part is hoping they remember who you are. Industry people can party pretty hard.

Ladies Night: Avoid Ladies Night like you would a creepy stranger with his johnson hanging out. These events are not the Playboy Mansion-esque hangs they seem; sure the drinks are cheap, but there's usually only one chick for every four dudes. Calling it "Ladies Night" is the biggest misnomer ever. This is bad for the fellas because the competition gets extra fierce, and it's bad for the ladies because that many horny guys competing with each other just makes the whole vibe fell kinda rapey. Just don't go.

Dress Codes: Any place that has a dress code is not gonna be cheap. Don't even bother. Plus, generally speaking, the dress codes are meant to keep out the thuggish riffraff who get drunk and get into fights. I'm willing to bet that just about every nightclub where someone gets shot has a dress code.

Go out on Weeknights: Here's the truth: going out to popular bars on weekend nights is like going to amateur hour. Too many people are blowing off steam, doing blow, and blowing each other. While all of those have their time and place, doing them on weekend nights means the main thing getting blown is your money. Since a lot places get weekend tourists (ie the "bridge and tunnel" crowds), really popular spots will either raise the price of their drinks, charge a cover, or both. This shitty college bar in Greenwich Village called Wicked Willy's does both of these. They literally raise the drink prices $3 on weekend nights. What the fuck, right?

So here's the answer: go out on weeknights. The earlier in the week you go out, like Monday or Tuesday, the better chance you have of scoring some sweet deals. Since we all inevitably go out on weekends, avoid trendy places and just find yourself some good dive bars. I'm not gonna say they'll treat you good, but they certainly won't shake you down.

Don't Go to Clubs: There is no stupider way of spending all your money than going out to clubs. Why on earth would you pay a steep cover charge to go in a place that then charges you grossly overinflated prices for drinks? Unless you're a douchebag, you don't. And if you are a douchebag, please stop being one.

Only a douchebag wants to be in a place where everyone is trying to prove how rich and awesome they are. Plus when people are showing off that much, their feelings get hurt real easily, which explains why there are always more fights at clubs than at bars.

I'm much more of a drinker than a dancer so I absolutely abhor going to clubs. Why would I want to go to some high-end place where the furniture is made by Nordic snowmen and the clientele consists of anorexic 17-year-old models drinking $15 Burberry-flavored Cosmos? But I occasionally have to go for some stupid reason or another. When that's the case I make sure that I'm somehow getting in for free and that I'm bringing a flask. You should, too.

Drink in Gay Bars: I don't give a fuck if you're gay or not. Gay bars have something for everyone. If you're gay or lesbian, you want to be here anyways. If you're a straight girl it's all the dancing you want without any of the weird grabby dudes. If you're a straight guy, you're the only available meat for a bunch of fruit flies who've spent all night dancing with attractive men who are absolutely unattainable. I have certainly met girls in gay bars before.

But here's the rub (actually that happens in the restroom), drinks are usually way cheaper than at non-gay bars. For example, there was a bar in San Francisco called Bar on Church that sold 80 cent drinks during their Monday 80's night. Yeah, you read that right, 80 cent drinks! At that price they should have handed out a condom with every third drink. But actually they didn't have to because every gay bar I've ever been in has jars of free condoms anyways. Cheap drinks, free condoms, and shitty dance music. Hey, at least two out of three ain't bad.

Drink in Dive Bars: I've always been a fan of shitty bars full of shitty people. The drinks are cheap, they're poured strong, and nobody cares what kind of depraved things you end up doing. Plus chances are you'll end up hearing some pretty incredible and strange stories as well. And yeah, the drinks are cheap. I know I already said that, but that's really why I go.

The Secret to Buying Rounds: Often times when you're out with some friends, people end up buying rounds for the whole group. This can get really expensive when it's your turn because, since everyone generally has different tastes in drinks, you buying a round for five people could very easily be more expensive than if you just bought yourself five drinks. If you drink well whiskey and your pal is drinking Johnny Walker Blue Label, you're gonna end up paying way more than you want to.

So here's the trick, don't offer to buy a round until you're all a few drinks in. Then the next time someone brings you a beverage, drink it really fast (but not so everyone notices) and then stand up and say, "I'm getting a drink, anybody want one?" Since everyone will still be only a quarter done with theirs, they'll all pass. You'll just have to buy your own, but when you get back to the table you'll still be included in the rounds that everyone else buys. I read about this trick years ago in some men's magazine and I can tell you it certainly works.

The Old Jell-O Trick: If you're going to some outdoors concert or festival where they allow you to bring in picnic items but not booze, make a tub of alcoholic gelatin shots. It's just like Jell-O shots but a big square instead of individual bits. The person checking bags will just think it's the dessert for your picnic, and be totally unaware that you're gonna get drunk off Jell-O.

Make Jungle Juice: Back when I was in college a couple guys I was friends with, Marc and Ed, used to rent out a place (I think for a joint birthday) and throw giant parties. Considering everyone attending was hovering just below age of 21, I'm surprised anyone actually rented to them, but that's a whole different story. Regardless, Marc and Ed used to always have a trashcan full of this super potent jungle juice that got everyone got super fucked up. There always ended up being quite a few people puking and I'm pretty sure one time I ended up having random unprotected sex in an alleyway when it was 45 degrees outside, so please be warned that jungle juice causes extremely poor decision making skills.

I recently friended Ed on Facebook and asked him what his recipe was all those years ago for that potion he always made. This was his answer, "I haven't thought about the jungle juice in years, but it was as simple as it gets. A Costco pack of frozen, concentrated juice mixed with as much alcohol as tolerable. And I use 'tolerable' very loosely." If my memory serves me right (and considering the circumstances, it probably doesn't) I think they used to mix that shit with a big ass oar. I know others mix the concentrate with half beer and half alcohol to make it go a little further and give people at least a chance to remember SOME of the night.

So, if you're having a party, jungle juice is a perfect way to get tons of people drunk for not a lot of money. Or I guess you can make a batch to keep in your fridge and take some in a flask with you when you go out. There are literally hundreds of recipes on the web that are a bit more specific than Ed's, so if you're looking to make some, check 'em out. Hangover guaranteed.

Brew Your Own Beer: Ever thought of brewing your own beer? It's not as a hard as it sounds, trust me, I've got some friends that are fucking morons that have been able to do it. Your start up costs ring in at about $100 but once you get going you'll be able to make a few cases of beer for you and your pals. Home brewing has been gaining major popularity in the past decade or so and home brew stores have popped up all over. Even if there isn't a home brew store in your town, there's bound to be a community and you can use ye olde internet to find out how to get involved. Just so you know though, your first few batches will probably be terrible. Sorry, that's just the way it goes.

How to Make Hobo Wine: Let's face it, unless you really wanna dedicate yourself to it, you're probably not going to be able to make a kick ass wine. Most of the people who do, land somewhere between idiot savants and alchemists, or they've given their entire lives over to winemaking. I have a feeling you're none of the above. But I came across this easy recipe for making cheap vino from grape juice, and when they called it "hobo wine" I knew it was for you and me. Now I'm not gonna transcribe the whole thing because 1. It would take up A LOT of room 2. I think that's called plagiarism and 3. Because I'm lazy. But it's all right here. Let me know how it turns out: wikihow.com/Brew-Cheap-Wine.

Go on Factory and Winery Tours: Paying for booze is silly when getting it for free just requires pretending you're interested in something you're not. Sure the processes of whiskey distillation, beer brewing, or wine making are kinda interesting, but you know what's even better? Getting drunk off those beverages! And you know what's even better than that? Getting drunk off those beverages for free! Generally speaking, most breweries and distilleries give tours highlighting the ways they make their delicious drinks. Some of them charge for the tours and some don't, but almost all let you get your beak wet at the end by giving you samples of their beverages. Another option for some free tipple is to go to the nearest wine region and take a tour. Many wineries let you taste A LOT of product hoping that you'll get drunk enough to actually bring some home. Enjoy!

Alcohol Promotions: Booze companies run alcohol promotions throughout the country on any given night of the week. Sometimes you have to play some dumb card game with the promo girl to get a free cocktail, others you just have to seem really excited to try whatever they're giving away. Most bars post signs about them or just ask the bartender if they have any coming up. If you live in a major city like NYC, Chicago, or San Francisco, sign up for the weekly My Open Bar newsletter (www.myopenbar.com) that lists exactly these once a week.

Best Hangover Cures

Even if you follow my rule of only drinking good vodka and soda, things can still go awry. The bartender or a friend could randomly buy you a few shots of Jack or you might get sick of drinking the same thing over and over again. Everybody has their own personal way of dealing with the horridness of being hungover, usually a combination of greasy food/hair of the dog/long shower/napping/laying on the couch watching *Law & Order* marathons.

I do this thing on BrokeAssStuart.com called "Broke-Ass of the Week". It's where we feature a different person from the community shedding a little light on their life of brokeitude. One question that is always asked is, "What's the best hangover cure". Below are some of my favorite answers. Thanks to Alison Lambert from BrokeAssStuart.com for giving me this idea:

Robert Reid – US Travel Editor for Lonely Planet (ReidOnTravel.blogspot.com): I gave up on hangovers a long time ago – no matter what, I seem to know when it's too much, when to stop. That said, I go to Russia sometimes. That means once or twice weekly of way too much alcohol. One time I woke up after a night of vomiting in the hall of my Siberian guesthouse filled with construction workers and found hangover tablets in my pocket. Someone had put them there the night before. Always drink with people who carry spares.

Tim Donnelly – Contributing editor to Brokelyn (Brokelyn.com): Soy chorizo wrap with Sriracha sauce, crinkle-cut wedge fries, salt and vinegar potato chips and prescription-grade migraine medication.

Patrick Hosmer – Animator (HeyMister.net): I had an exchange student from England once and his hangover cure was to buy a loaf of bread at a bakery, tear off one end and hollow it out, slather the inside with ketchup and then fill it with potato chips. It's not that. Any permutation of a sausage, egg and cheese will do me right. Black coffee. People shutting up.

Sigmund Amadeus Werndorf – Owner of the best name ever: A full on, traditional Irish breakfast. Nothing drives out the hangover better then three kinds of meat, three kinds of carbohydrates, and no fruit or vegetables.

Chris – Founder of The Skint (TheSkint.com): Drink a ton of water before you go to sleep, and for god's sake don't drink without eating dinner (reminder to self).

Kelly Malone – Founder of the SF Indie Mart (Indie-Mart. com) and Workshop (WorkShopSF.org): Ashamed to admit it, but a McDonald's double cheeseburger, a Revive Vitamin Water, 2 Flintstones vitamins and a ton of aspirin.

Mike Force – Illustrator and designer of this book (AutoTone.net): Odwalla's Superfood and a very long walk. I once had a hangover that wouldn't stop unless I was walking, so I walked for hours.

Matt Haney – Founder of Citizen Hope (CitizenHope.org): Kombucha. I have no idea what is in those things, but any drink that has living things inside of it has to be able to work magic. If anything the little sea monkeys in there will give new life to whatever the alcohol has destroyed.

Jeff Cleary – Stand Up Comic: I've devoted most of my life to the scientific research of this subject. If you're lucky, you'll remember to have a glass of water after every 3rd drink. If it's too late and you wake up with a monster hangover the only thing I've found that works is a long hot shower. Just linger in there for a while and let the water run off your head, then go back to bed. Old, obese cats are great for hangovers, too. They're always game for sleeping it off, which is great.

Todd Montesi – Stand up comic: A cup of tea usually works. Followed by jerking off. And weeping. Then death. It's the David Carradine cocktail (too soon or too late for that reference?).

Lawrence Bonk – Song writer: I usually just end up in bed chanting "oh God" over and over until it passes, which doesn't happen for many, many hours. The part of my brain that is able to rationalize things positively shuts down during a hangover.

Kevin Montgomery – Founder of Uptown Almanac (UptownAlmanac.com): Shut your mouth and deal with it.

Kelli Rudick – One of my favorite musicians (Myspace.com/KelliRudick): There's no hangover if you simply sleep through the next day entirely.

Julia Wertz – The girl behind Fart Party (FartParty.org): Just keep on drinkin'

How to Make Your Own
Coffee-Flavored Liquor (similar to Kahlúa)
By Oliver Hartman (OliverHartman.com)

I know I'm a friggin' pinch when I deny myself White Russians because of the price of Kahlúa. And goddammit, sometimes I don't wanna drink my vodka neat, chased by a pickle, like an actual white Russian. But let's be honest, there is more to Kahlúa than The Dude. Kahlúa was one of the few things my puritanical mother would drink (only in the summer, with my aunt, in the form of sombreros: Kahlúa and milk). And it got a non-drinking Nicaraguan friend of mine off the wagon (he only drinks it straight).

2 cups water

1 ½ cup dark brown sugar

1 ½ cup granulated sugar

½ cup instant coffee crystals

1.75 liters shitty vodka

2 teaspoons vanilla extract

1 whole vanilla bean (optional)

Remove cap from vanilla extract and inhale. Damn, it smells so good! Fight vanilla withdrawal and combine all your sugar with your water in a saucepan and simmer for approximately 12-15 minutes. The important thing is that the sugar has dissolved. This will look like baby diarrhea. Take your baby diarrhea off the heat and stir in your instant coffee crystals. Let the caffeinated poo mix cool completely.

Pour the cooled mix into a large plastic container with a lid or a big ass bottle(s) you have lying around (wash it thoroughly, and sterilizing it with boiling water can't hurt) and get ready to mix in your vodka and vanilla elements.

Take a huge shot of straight vodka as a quality control measure.

Stir in vodka and vanilla elements with the cooled baby poo. This brew can age anywhere from a week to a few months. Sample it before you go to work to determine its readiness.

How to Infuse Your Own Vodka
By Amber Bouman (AmberBouman.com)

Vodka is a complex mistress. One minute she's lovin' up on ya, and you're the suave, classy chick drinking vodka martinis and charming strangers. The next morning you're on your bathroom floor with eyeliner gobs in the corner of your eyes, wearing one shoe and hating life. However, vodka is a perfect summertime drink because she plays well with such a grand variety of mixers. Got juices (Cranberry, Grapefruit, Orange)? Vodka. Soda (7-Up, Ginger Ale, Grape Drink)? Vodka. Veggie Juice? Vodka. Milk? Vodka. And, as if that wasn't already enough to make Miss V a VIP, vodka can be infused with a variety of flavors which is not only sorta fun but also ridiculously easy to do. How ridiculously easy? It really only requires three steps:

• pick a flavor

• stick what makes that flavor in a jar with a lot of vodka

and cap the jar

• stick your jar of flavor/vodka mix somewhere cool and dry for a few weeks

• drink

Seriously, it's not a lot more complicated than that. I myself tried out the idea after seeing it in an old issue of some magazine. So, you'll need to pick a flavor (grapefruit? vanilla-plum? jalapeño? berry-cinnamon?) and wash any fruits. Obviously the more ingredients, the stronger the flavor but the more space in the jar filled with say, apples, the less space you have for vodka.

Experience shows that aiming for two items of larger fruits (like apples or apricots) or 2-4 fistfuls of smaller fruits (like berries) or 1-2 fistfuls of fresh herbs or 1 fistful of dried herbs is what you should use. Fruits gets sliced (remove pits, seeds, stems), berries get bruised, and herbs get crushed gently to release flavor. Grab a clean mason jar (get these from a hardware store or grocery store if you don't already have a few laying around), toss your ingredients in, fill 'er up with vodka and then seal it. Put it somewhere dry and cool and away from sunlight, like a cabinet or closet. Now leave it the eff alone for about a week. Stronger flavors like citrus may infuse sooner (2-5 days) but softer things like ginger or vanilla will take longer. I used blood oranges and did a taste-test at about 7 days; I wound up putting it back into the closet for another week or so.

After it was done infusing, I stuck it in the freezer. Done-zo! Added bonus: the mason jar makes for extremely easy carrying to movies, parks, bbq's, rooftop parties, bingo nights at church, and bonfires. How to Never Get Hung Over: I've actually solely started drinking Ketel One and soda. Now look, I know that's not exactly broke-ass, but follow me for a sec. Ketel-sodas are only like 6 bucks at the bars I go to so I end up spending like around $12 ($2 extra per drink) more than I would've if I'd been drinking well vodka all night. But here's the thing: if I only drink Ketel-sodas all night long, I get absolutely no hangover! Amazing right? So next time you're disgustingly hungover, think about whether or not you'd pay $12 to not be hungover. I just pulled a logical checkmate on your ass.

How To Build Your Home Bar
By Sarah M. Smart (SarahMSmart.com)

It's high time we discussed drinking at home in more depth. Getting hammered in bars is all well and good, especially if you can get someone else to buy your drinks. But then you always end up owing somebody something. So clearly the way to save money – and make friends! – is by boozin' it up at your place.

BroKe-Ass Porn

40's

Nothing says "I'm broke as shit, but I still wanna party!" quite like a 40 ounce bottle of malt liquor. Whether your particular potion is Mickey's, St. Ides, Olde English, Colt 45, or Steel Reserve, having a 40 in your hand shows the world that being "classy" just isn't your thing.

I distinctly remember my first 40. It was back in the days when Death Row Records ruled the charts and every sixteen year old boy's rap video fantasy was to be at a party where the fridge was filled with nothing but malt liquor. I was probably 15 at the time and shared a bottle of Mickey's with three of my buddies at a bonfire at La Jolla Shores in San Diego. Back then we were never able to finish the bottle; we drank slowly enough that the last three fingers worth always got too warm.

Today, almost 15 years later, I salute the venerable 40 oz for single handedly making every house party, bonfire, and day in the park, that much better.

Do you remember your first 40?

Bar Basics

First, know when to be spendy and when to be thrifty. If you primarily want to make mixed drinks, there's no need to go top-shelf. However, if you like to sip on a snifter of brandy or a neat bourbon, don't take your chances on those no-name liquors. Bottles of decent booze seem a bit pricey, but you'll feel better when you think about how much you're saving (one Captain and Coke at home costs less than $1, whereas it's $4 at the bar in the best-case scenario). If you have friends of means, consider throwing a liquor party: You provide beer, wine, and munchies, and everyone else must bring a bottle of their favorite alcoholic libation. Here's what you'll need before you can start calling it a home bar:

Vodka: Trader Joe's sells a huge bottle of something called "Vodka of the Gods" for $10, and since nobody (in their right mind) drinks straight vodka, it doesn't matter what you buy.

Gin: I'm not a big gin drinker, but it's helpful to have some Tanqueray or Bombay Sapphire around for any old, English gentlemen you might entertain.

Rum: A white rum, like Bacardi, and a spiced rum, such as Captain Morgan, should meet most of your rum needs.

Whiskey: This broad category technically also includes bourbons and scotches. In my opinion, the best whiskey to cover all your bases is Jameson. It's also not too expensive: $20 for a normal-sized bottle.

Tequila: Everybody knows tequila turns you into a screaming, punching, crying nightmare, so maybe get a lower-quality one, such as Jose Cuervo, expressly for making margaritas.

Triple sec: Also great in margaritas, any ol' brand of triple sec will add that orangey flavor to your drinks.

Schnapps: Mmm, schnapps. Peach appears in drink recipes most often, but consider picking up a few other flavors depending on your personal preferences.

Other liqueurs: You can get as many or as few as you like. Think about what you tend to order when you're at the bar: Fernet? Jägermeister? Goldschläger? Stores sell any number of disgusting things!

Beer and wine: Dude, you know what to do. Have a 12-pack of lager on hand to satiate almost any guest. Drop a few bones on a bottle each of chardonnay and cabernet sauvignon that you'll probably never drink, as well. Can't be too prepared!

Tools of the Trade

By now, you're probably staring blankly at your bottles of Rumple Minze, Baileys, and Everclear, wondering, "What on earth do I do now?" Two options:

1) SHOTS (what are you, 15?) and
2) get some tools to help you mix sophisticated drinks:

Citrus press: I thought I was cool squeezing lemons by hand for my sidecars, but then a total sweetheart gifted me a citrus press, and it has changed my life. It gets all the juice that your hand or your ordinary hand juicer misses – and keeps it seed-free. I can't figure a way to DIY something that works this well, but it's really not that expensive anyway. Plus it flattens your lime half in a really cute way so it's almost inside-out.

Cocktail shaker and strainer: Of course you can buy these, but it's super-easy to jerry-rig a couple of glasses. Grab two glasses out of the mismatched set you found on the sidewalk, and make sure that one is slightly smaller in circumference than the other. When you're shaking to mix a cocktail, pour your ingredients and ice in the bigger glass, invert the small one on top (snugly!), hold the edges together, and shake away! When you're ready to strain out the ice, flip the small glass so the two glasses are facing the same direction, and use that to hold the ice at bay as you pour into a repurposed peanut butter jar. Classy!

Shot glasses: Or use some really tiny jars; just make sure it holds about one ounce. Shot glasses are good for measuring in addition to getting drunker faster.

Muddler: Don't have a muddler for your mojito? Do you have a big mixing spoon? The edge of the spoon is thick enough for muddling purposes. Just jam it against the mint in the bottom of your glass until it looks sufficiently broken up.

Regular ol' flatware: Need a spoon to get cherries from the jar? Use… a spoon. Should a guest request a stirred martini rather than shaken, well, a butter knife is long enough to reach the bottom of most glasses. I can't think of any good bar uses for forks, though – help a sister out?

Corkscrew and bottle opener: Again, you know what to do. The corkscrew is for wine, and the bottle opener is for any bottle that isn't a twist-off. If you have any interest whatsoever in recreational alcohol consumption, you should already have both of these. But if you're in a pinch, there's a way to open a bottle of beer using another bottle of beer. So meta.

Mixers and More

If you want to be a bar star, you'll need a couple more things so you can have that fancy cocktail party without being laughed out of town.

Booze is terrifically yummy (and effective!) by itself, but not everyone likes it neat (that's code for "plain and room-temperature"). We'll call them "pussies." I'm a pussy myself, in fact; I'd much prefer to be taking my vodka in the company of some grapefruit juice, for example. Therefore, I and many other borderline alcoholics find that certain mixers and other ingredients are necessary. Remember, a spoonful of sugar helps the medicine go down. Take note:

Pop: Or soda, or coke, or whatever you heathens call it. We'll need some cola, some ginger ale, Sprite or one of its many knockoffs, club soda (aka sparkling water at Trader Joe's), and tonic. Juice: orange, grapefruit, cranberry, pineapple, tomato, and whatever else you can get your hands on. Some people like to foray into Clamato territory, but I personally find that disgusting.

Flavors: I wasn't really sure what to call this category, but it basically consists of (duh) ingredients you might use to flavor your drinks. You might want to hook up with some bitters as well as some sour mix. DIY this by stirring together one part each of sugar, water, lime juice, and lemon juice. Finally, keep your pantry on hand: salt, sugar, hot sauce, whipped cream, etc.

Garnishes: Some actually enhance the flavors of your drinks! Green olives, tiny onions if that's your thing (and if it's not, you hate cute things and therefore you hate AMERICA), citrus fruits, ginger, maybe some fresh herbs, celery or other weird things you like to put in bloody marys, and –my favorite! – maraschino cherries. I could eat those ripe, red, sweet harbingers of happiness all goddamn day.

Drink mixes: for when you're extra-lazy! They make margarita mix, bloody mary mix, Long Island mix, daiquiri mix... Some of them even come with the alcohol already in them! Could things possibly be any better? Salty snacks: Not an essential for making a drink, but you know people wanna get their drunchies (drunk munchies) on once they knock a few back. In the absence of classy hors d'oeuvres, buy a jar of peanuts or a bag of pretzels to keep on hand. Better yet, invest in a popcorn machine! What could possibly go wrong?

A place to keep all this crap: Mini-fridge? Regular fridge? An actual bar? A dedicated space in your cabinet? It's just nice to keep all your booze and extras in one spot for ease and style. I got the service cart that houses my bottles and tools from a sidewalk.

Stretch That Booze, Son!

At this point, your home bar should be nearing completion. You've likely dropped a month's burrito money on stocking your shelves with the booze, the tools, and the other essentials, but it'd be a crime for me to turn you loose now. Now let's going to chat about getting more for your money and making your materials last longer:

Buy single servings of bubbly mixers. Unlike juice, which doesn't have any carbonation to lose, club soda and other pops will turn flat if you don't use the entire bottle in short order after opening. Play it safe by purchasing cans or small bottles of cola and club soda and by getting juice in family-sized containers.

Switch to the cheaper stuff once you're buzzed. Did someone else bring a bottle of no-name whisky to your party? Bust it out; you shouldn't be able to taste the difference by now.

Mix, mix, mix. Even stuff that you don't think should be mixed. You're obviously drinking more liquid, so it tricks your brain into thinking you've had a lot more. It also (ideally) takes a longer time to drink, so it slows you down. Do you think mixing wine with club soda or champagne with orange juice is a crime? Do you like buying a new box of Franzia every day?

Snacks. Your food approach when drinking is crucial to how much you'll drink. If you want your booze to last longer, that means you want to get drunk on less. Sure, doctors don't advise this, but drinking on an empty stomach works. However, it comes with its own set of challenges and regrets (HANGOVER ALERT).

Ration. Set up some kind of system that forces you to take some time between your drinks. Have a glass of water after each drink, or hit the bathroom, or make the social circuit. Also, apply the mindful eating technique to your drinking: Really experience and enjoy each sip you take. Live in the moment, you hippie boozer. This will also keep you from getting too drunk, grabbing your roommate's ass, and waking up with puke in your hair.

If a drink sucks, don't throw it out; that's money you're dumping down the drain. If it's not strong enough, add more booze (duh). If it's too strong, add more of your mixer(s). If you hate the flavor, that's a little trickier, but sour mix and cherries can solve even the nastiest drink problems!

Last resort: Moderation. No success implementing any of these tips? Well, all I can say to you – sad, sorry, broke fuck that you are – is "drink less."

The Proof Is in the John Collins

Congratulations, you've made it to the end of my home-bar tutorial! This means you've got the ingredients, the tools, and the know-how to build your liquor cabinet and entertain imbibing guests – or just yourself! So now you can reap the rewards: HUGE SAVINGS! Plus nobody will throw you out of your own home for being wasted!

I told you that you'd save money by drinking at home rather than at bars, so now I have to prove it. I'm going to list my favorite drinks, how I'd make them (cost will vary based on how strong you like your drinks and what liquor you use), what they'd cost on average at a bar without any kind of special promotion (e.g., happy hour) in effect and not including tip, what they'll cost to make at home per drink, and how much you save (N.B. I had to do a lot of research and math to figure these out, so forgive me if any of these figures are a tad off):

Whiskey sour: glassful of ice + 1 shot Jameson + sour mix

- Bar: $8
- Home: $0.95
- You save: $7.05, or 88%

Cape Cod: glassful of ice + 1 shot well vodka + cranberry juice

- Bar: $6
- Home: $0.89
- You save: $5.11, or 85%

Greyhound: glassful of ice + 2 shots well vodka + grapefruit juice

Bar: $6
Home: $0.90
You save: $5.10, or 79%

Gin and tonic: glassful of ice + 1 shot Tanqueray + tonic water

- Bar: $9
- Home: $2.07
- You save: $6.93, or 85%

Pina colada: a shit-ton of ice + Mr. and Mrs. T's Pina Colada Mix (high five for laziness!) + 1 shot Malibu (you'll need a blender)

- Bar: $10 (extra charge for inconveniencing the bartender)
- Home: $2.27
- You save: $7.73, or 77%

Martini: glassful of ice + 1 shot Tanqueray + a few drops of vermouth

• Bar: $9
• Home: $1.40
• You save: $7.60, or 84%

Margarita: glassful of ice + salted rim + 2 shots well tequila + 1 shot triple sec + juice of 1 lime

• Bar: $6
• Home: $1.73
• You save: $4.27, or 71%

Glass of cabernet sauvignon: 1 bottle of Charles Shaw wine

• Bar: $6
• Home: $0.50
• You save: $5.50, or 92%

Shot of Wild Turkey: 1 bottle of Wild Turkey

• Bar: $8
• Home: $0.50
• You save: $7.50, or 94%, plus any pride you have left

Now you are ready, young, alcoholic grasshopper, to unleash your mad mixology upon the world and drink more cheaply– and more often – than ever before! Good luck, drink responsibly, never drink and drive, and all the rest of that stuff. Most important, have fun!

If anyone ever puts out an album compilation called "Hipster Love Songs" this totally needs to be the album cover

Dating for Broke-Asses

Dating, the biggest breaker of hearts, egos, and banks. Lucky for you, I've put together a little guide to make sure you never have an empty wallet or bed.

Meeting People to Date

Look around: You are surrounded by people doing the same things you do every day, and one of those people might even share your weird obsession with pictures of cats wearing wigs. The grocery store, the library, the subway, the coffee cart, record stores, book stores–next time you're doing what you do, take off your headphones and look up from your smart phone. I'm not saying you should start giving people the creepy eye as you try to imagine what your children would look like, just be approachable and make a non-threatening, normal comment like "Sorry to bother you, but wondering if you know anything about this book/record/jar of mushrooms?" if you feel like it would appropriate. And only if you can do it without heavy breathing and developing pit stains.

Go to things you're interested in, and go alone: Rolling solo ups your approachability factor big time. Going up to talk to one girl or guy seems feasible for other people, going up to talk to two girls or guys makes you the other person the third wheel. But going out alone can be a major cause of anxiety for some people, which is why it helps to go to things that you'll geek out about enough to feel excited to be there anyways. Science Club nights, cooking demonstrations, book lectures... it works best to pick an event that features a non-talking portion followed by a talking portion, so you can pull topics from the event (or bounce if you decide you're not up for it).

Here are some things/places to try:

• Watch sports games at a bar. Automatic shared interest and conversation starter, plus social lubricant.

• Check out special interest clubs and events like Science Night, Book Clubs, Chili Aficionados, etc

• Meet Up Groups on Meetup.com

• Concerts. Go early and grab a drink at the bar, or talk to other people waiting in line

• Volunteer

• Free Classes

• Join a sporting league

There are now cards that even make the awkward introductions for you now–**FlipMe** (FlipMe.com) and **Cheek'd** (cheekd.com). Basically, dole out a card ranging from the tame "Hi. You've been Cheek'd" to FlipMe's "I'm playing Easy to Get," and assuming the other person isn't the average lazy person/too drunk to hold on to the card/extremely unattracted to you, they will go online and check your ish out. These cost money, and the other person might be annoyed they have to sign up online to talk to you when they could have just talked to you the other night in person, but if this seems up your alley give it a go and let me know how it goes.

Be bold: If you see someone you wanna talk to, just go for it. The worst thing they can do is reject you. And knowing that they aren't interested is way better than spending the rest of your life wondering. Also, one thing I learned a long time ago is not to get discouraged if you get shot down. Just because one person isn't into you doesn't mean the next person won't be. Everyone has different tastes. Just think about how awful some of your friends' significant others are. I mean, they're fucking terrible, right?

Treat dating like looking for a job. If you're serious about meeting someone, tell your friends you're looking and what you're looking for just like you would if you were looking for employment. If they like you, they are almost guaranteed to help. There will inevitably be some disaster set-ups but there will also be terrific ones. Just be careful not to take it too personally if there are more of the former and get paranoid about what your friend must think of you if they set you up with an asshole. Personalities rub against each other different ways in different settings, so the date who wouldn't stop making fun of your shirt could actually be awesome to sit next to at work.

Investigate your social circles. Our lives, and our friends' lives, are now documented on this wee little thing called Facebook. If you are the average person, you have already Facebook-stalked at some point today, so why not try to get a date out of it?

Here's how to use FB's most basic tools for dating ranked in order of least to most awkward

Facebook Events: Check out who else is being roped into your friend's art opening before you go, just make sure not to bring up the fact you did this as a way to introduce yourself no matter how much free wine you guzzle.

Friend's Photos: Your friends wouldn't post pictures to Facebook if they didn't want you to look at them. So look at them, then casually inquire about any hot new faces you find and the prospect of them sleeping with you at some point. I know a handful of (successful!) relationships that have started this way.

Friend Browser: Just type in a Facebook friend's name, click the "Friends" section in their profile and BAM, instant access to friends of friends you could knock boots with. Because everyone's gotten hip to the whole privacy setting thing, you'll likely have to use an unsuspecting way of asking about them to your shared friend.

Facebook Friending: Some people are all 'Gimme Gimme!' when it comes to more FB friends, so why not try to give them one more? Now that FB suggests you be friends with anyone you share a friend or two with, it's significantly less awkward to friend someone you don't know but think you could make out with after a margarita or two.

Facebook Poke: Actually maybe don't do this. "Are they poking me ironically? Are they poking me because they want to, um, poke me?" It never stops being confusing and weird.

Facebook Messaging: This is a lot like passing a note in high school. You know whatever you write is going to be shown to at least 5 of the other person's friends, so pick your words carefully.

Facebook Ad: For around $20, you can make your own modern day personal ad. Definitely think this one through because someone you know is definitely going to find out about this and taunt you forever for turning your life into the movie *Must Love Dogs*.

Facebook Dating Applications: Seems folks have gotten hip to ye olde 'Book's matchmaking potential and introduced applications to help you scoot right along.

iWould: The app allows you to go through your friend list and select 1-10 people you'd make out with if the situation should present itself. The application cross-references your list with those of your friends also using the app. If someone you selected put you on their list, you'll both get a notice of the match. This actually seems promising.

Zoosk, Are You Interested?, Badoo, and SpeedDate are others but don't forget that as with any app, you're allowing a third party to tap into your Facebook information.

Organized Dating

OK, so maybe Facebook stalking or sipping a cappuccino at a coffee shop while hoping someone comes up to talk to you about your band t-shirt seems a little douchey to you. Or maybe you just know that you will probably not be able to successfully talk to a stranger while deciding if you want to have sex with them or not. Fortunately most people feel this way, so you are not destined for a life watching *SNL* on Saturday nights alone with Bagel Bites crumbs all over your chest after all.

Speed Dating: It's the *8 Minute Abs* of dating! Basically, you have eight minutes to make a good impression on a stranger. This will be fantastic or a disaster depending on how awkward and ugly you are.

Singles Meet Up Groups: Meetup.com is an awesome way to meet other people who have the same odd affinities as you, and is also host to tons of singles groups across the country.

Craigslist: Great for bed frames, bad for bed friends. Please don't use Craigslist to date.

Online Dating: According to market research at the time this book was written, 1 out of 6 current marriages happening in the US originated online, and nearly 30% of couples meet on the internet. What CAN'T the Internet do!? No wonder there are a shit ton of online dating options to choose from.

It's hard to say if one is better than the other because that depends on who is using them in your area. In New York City, **OKCupid.com** and **Nerve.com** are extremely popular. *The Onion* even has its own personals (which I thought definitely seemed like a joke until a staffer informed me otherwise). Some other free sites are Mingles.com, Connectingsingles.com, PlentyOfFish.com, Singlesnet.com,Zoosk. com. Gay? You're not alone—check out Adam4Adam.com.

There are others that have an interesting spin, such as **Great Boyfriends** (GreatBoyfriends.com) where non-grudge holding exes of girlfriends and boyfriends can recommend their former flames. **How About We** (HowAboutWe.com) is a more casual take on the whole cyber dating scene, where you basically just propose a date you'd like to go on and hope someone else wants to too (example "How about we... sniff some paint and watch Ghostbusters while making out on my couch?).

Some sites are super specific like **Date My Pet** (DateMyPet.com) for pet lovers (ahem...cat ladies), **Humordate** (HumorDate.com) for self-proclaimed "funny people" as in, many of your dates will probably be the other person's open mic night, or the Atlasphere (TheAtlasphere.com) for fans of Ayn Rand. Yes, you read that correctly, and I'm sure there's some kind of test to make sure you're pretentious enough before you can join. Twitter even has its own dating service–Luv@FirstTweet (LoveAtFirstTweet.com) --which honestly kind of sounds like a nightmare but give it a go if you're into conversations of 140 characters or less.

Virtual Vanity

So after you finally pick an online dating services (or several, why the hell not?) next you gotta prove you're actually worth talking to. Here are some tips to help you survive the search:

Pick a username that's normal. Don't try to seem smart by quoting an obscure reference from your favorite 19th century short story, or try to seem sexy. You will probably come across as the opposite of what you're trying to.

Don't Lie in Your Profile. No matter how big or small your lie is, the truth will prevail and you will look like a jerkoff. Also, don't write a novel, and make sure to spell check.

Keep Your Photo Recent & Real. The idea behind online dating is to meet one of these people in person one day, and people aren't nice enough to keep going out with you once they realize you Photoshopped out your snaggletooth.

Update Your Profile Regularly. Dating sites often bump most recently updated accounts to the top of the search engine heap.

Don't Be Stupid. Would you give a stranger hitting on you at a bar your personal, hackable, life-ruining private information? Nope. Same applies here.

Be Patient. The internet moves fast, but not always that fast.

Making Contact

All online services have their own weird little cues and games for showing people you're interested. Winks, waves, whatever–you have to figure that part out by seeing what other people are doing. But inevitably, you will be ready for the first step: the email.

Email Tip #1: Are You Really Compatible? Before you write that first response, decide if you actually would have a good time with this person.

Email Tip #2: Be prepared. Read the person's profile, understand it, and reference it.

Email Tip #3: Keep it simple. Don't overwhelm them with paragraphs describing your weird fetishes and the scarring experience you had that one time you went to Aunt Edna's house. Start soft and slow so they don't feel like it's a chore to read or write back.

Email Tip #4: Keep it clean. Save the kinky talk for later in the game.

Email Tip #5: Watch out for email misunderstandings. Some of the best things in the world, like sarcasm, just don't translate well.

Dating Etiquette

You did it! You convinced someone you are worth spending time with. Here's how not to screw it up and disappoint your mom again.

Guidelines for first date survival

Make the first date something enjoyable with or without the other person. That way if the other person is terrible, it won't be a complete waste of time.

Prepare backup. Have a friend call or text you after 30 minutes into the date, or just pretend that they did. An easy out is saying your roommate is locked out. BAM. Bye, dud.

Have fake plans for after in case you need to cut it short.

Don't talk about exes. It's even wise to have a quick sentence synopsis about your dating past that's short, sweet, and doesn't allude to the fact you cried into your pillow every night for 3 years.

Guy or Gal, don't expect the other person to get the check. Go splitsies unless one person really really really wants to get it to avoid the fake polite "no no no" tango.

Conversation

These days Gemini & Scorpio (GeminiAndScorpio.com) may be one of the best and biggest underground event email lists in NYC, but it started off as a great online dating guide put together by two sharp and clever ladies. Even if their focus has changed, I highly recommend joining their email list if you live in the NYC area because it will keep you hip to a plethora of things you wouldn't hear about otherwise.

One great thing Gemini & Scorpio did is come up with this list of conversation starters to get things moving on a date. Check it out in their Guide to Online dating.

Drunk Dialing and Texting

It's best to come up with an action plan in advance to avoid showing up on "Texts from Last Night" or entering a ramble spiral resembling Mikey in *Swingers*. Fortunately, technology is on your side: applications like Designated Dialer, iDrunk Dialer, Bad Decision Blocker, and Don't Dial give you the chance to create a list of contacts to block and save from your 3:30AM shout out. The only thing better would be if my phone had a breathalizer.

Gmail's even in on the game and created Undo Send, so you can cancel accidentally embarrassing emails, and Mail Goggles, which forces you to solve a puzzle before you can send an email during certain times.

Long Distance Dating

Anna G. has been running the Sex and Dating column on BrokeAssStuart.com pretty much since the site started. So I figured I'd hand it over to her for a second and let her lay down some knowledge about Long Distance Dating:

Long Distance Dating by Anna G.

I am and always have been really against long distance relationships. They're either unbearably torturous or completely pointless, or maybe both. Sometimes, though, you find yourselves the victims of circumstance, and you just kind of have to deal with it. But how to deal? Here are my nuggets of wisdom:

1) Think long and hard if this shit makes any sense whatsoever

If you don't have any real plans to ever be together in the same city... like EVER, it kind of begs the question: what's the point? I mean, I guess if this type of relationship is fulfilling on both ends, then go for it. But if either of you aren't totally happy, then it's ridiculous to try and fool yourselves, no matter how much you legitimately care for the person.

2) There needs to be incredibly clear rules with regards to seeing other people

Because god help you if you break the rules. God. Help. You. As far as being able to see other people versus not being able to see other people and all the complexities therein, respectively, that's for you guys to decide. All I'm saying is that it might be unreasonable, depending on the amount of time and the total length of relationship, to expect people to remain celibate. That's all I'm going to say.

3) Don't make crazy and rash decisions with regards to the level of your relationship

If you probably wouldn't get married (or move in together, or whatever) right now, it's most likely not a great idea to rush into it because you feel pressured that you or your significant other is leaving, or you feel like you can't go on living anymore if you continue to be apart from them. If something doesn't work out timing-wise, that's just the way it goes sometimes. Don't try to force shit because you think you'll never meet anyone like them again. You most likely will. There are tons of people in the world. And even if you don't meet anyone you remotely like for the rest of your life, who fucking cares? At least you didn't ruin your life for someone else.

4) Don't become a weird hermit

Just because you're sad you can't be with your significant other, it doesn't mean you can't have fun with OTHER people you care about. If you lock yourself up in your room every weekend, you'll just alienate yourself from everyone who actually IS there and create a weird co-dependent relationship with your absent partner. Plus, not everyone can pull off that long beard and cloak look.

5) Maybe that kiss between you and that random other person, that you can't get out of your head, really *does* mean something

Listen, none of us are perfect. As long as one makes a valiant effort to respect other people, and listen to your feelings, that's all anyone can ever ask of one. Maybe that kiss between you and Brody or whoever means that you really DO like Brody, or maybe it just means you're not as into Marco in Vancouver as much as you thought you were. I just thought I'd use name examples from the imaginary teen drama I made up in my head.

6) If at all possible, do not assign a sentimental indie rock song to your relationship

Because you will never, ever be able to listen to that song again without bursting out in tears and/or cringing. Ever. Sense memory is a sadistic and cliched sonofabitch.

How to Date on the Cheap

Whether you're looking for love or just a little lovin', dating can be a pretty expensive endeavor. But just because you're broke doesn't necessarily mean you have to stay at home all night looking at internet porn (unless that's your thing of course). There's a million ways you can take someone out on the town without having to spend all your loot (besides, do you really want to date someone who only cares about $100 dinners?).

Museum Free Days: For some reason, being smart and cultured is considered sexy. Whether you actually are these things doesn't really matter as long as you pretend to be, or at least pretend to want to be. And that's where museum free days come in. Pretty much all of the best museums in the United States have one or more days a month where admission is either free or "pay what you can" (for those of you who aren't too good with subtly, "pay what you can" means ignoring the disapproving looks the ticket taker gives you when you pay with a $1 bill). By taking your date to the museum on one of these days, you're not only saving money, you seem like you know *things* about *stuff*. That being said, spending a quiet day at the museum may not always be the best idea for a first date.

I remember a few years back meeting a girl at a bar and totally hitting it off with her. A couple days later we made plans to go to the SF MoMA for it's free day. Unfortunately for me, in the drunkenness of our first meeting, I didn't realize how quiet the girl was. All of this was fine during our time in the museum because you're *supposed* to be quiet there, but once we left the MoMA and went to the park across the street, she still didn't say much more than a few words at a time. Being the jabber mouth that I am, I couldn't handle all the dead air in our conversation, so I found myself talking even more than normal. I'd start saying shit I didn't even believe, just to avoid the awkwardness of her not saying anything. I'd be like, "Wow that Jackson Pollock piece was really quite amazing. Wasn't it?" and then think to myself, "Wait, I hated that fucking piece! What the hell am I talking about?".

I guess that story really didn't help illuminate my point about free museum days at all, but I figured that I'd include it anyway just because it happened on one of them. If nothing else you can at least

walk away from this having learned that, while free museum days are a good, cheap date, the quietness of the museum might mask the fact that the person you're with is either a mute or enjoys watching you squirm with awkwardness. In that case, maybe it was the best date she'd ever been on.

Museum Follow Up: Assuming the date didn't go down in flames after you accidentally knocked over and destroyed that priceless Faberge Egg, a good follow up to the museum would be having cheap booze and a picnic. Since most major museums are in central areas of cities, and therefore near parks, bring what you need for the picnic in a backpack. Once you get out of that quiet place with all the art, you can be as loud as you want and chug that booze you'd been thinking about the whole time. Two Buck Chuck from Trader Joe's is always a good bet if you're feeling classy, but I always tend to opt for a 40 oz. I guess you might wanna consult with your date beforehand to see which they prefer. I've been told you're supposed to have food at a picnic too, but I never make it past the Olde English 800.

Top Ten Free Museum Days in the USA

Despite having *some* super powers, I'm not omnipotent (yet), so I have no idea where you are. Therefore, I'd like to give you a list of the ten best free museum days (in no particular order) so that hopefully you can make it to whichever one is closest to you. Just remember to try to save the booze for after you leave the museum.

The Smithsonian – Washington DC: It's hard to get better than The Smithsonian. Not only are there 19 Smithsonian Museums, including the Air and Space Museum and a zoo, they are all free, all the time! You can take a different date to a different museum for almost three weeks straight. If you're having sex with all of them, make sure to use protection and send me photos.

The Field Museum – Chicago: The Second Monday of every month is free at Chicago's brilliant Field Museum. Sitting on Lake Michigan, the museum is filled with all kinds of awesome stuff like dinosaur skeletons, Native American artifacts, and lots of taxidermy. Taxidermy is sweet. www.fmnh.org/plan_visit/free_days.htm

Indianapolis Children's Museum – Indianapolis: Whether you knocked up your girl a couple years ago and now have a rug-rat, have a thing for nannies, or are just a kid at heart, the Indianapolis Children's Museum is a is a great place to be. This is especially the case the first Thursday of the month from 4-8pm, because that's when it's free.

The de Young Museum – San Francisco: The first Tuesday of the month is free at San Francisco's recently reopened fine arts museum. If your thing is indigenous and Oceanic art, then you're in luck. If not, don't worry. They got paintings too.

The Museum of Fine Arts – Houston: While Shell Oil may be among those responsible for global warming, they're also the ones responsible for free Thursdays at this museum. I'm not saying you should steal a Renoir from the museum, but if you do, see if you can put it on Shell's tab.

The Experience Music Project | Science Fiction Hall of Fame – Seattle: From the Frank Gehry building to the monorail to the actual exhibits, everything in these museums is fucking rad! Seriously. To see for yourself, check out the free admission and live music they offer from 5:00pm to 8:00pm on the first Thursday of the month during their winter hours schedule. www.empsfm.org/programs

Los Angeles County Museum of Art – Los Angeles: With over 150,000 works of art in its collection, there is a grip of shit to see here. I guess that's why they have so many free days. Besides it being "pay what you can" every day after 5pm (LA County residents only), they are also free to all on the second Tuesday of the month. But that's not all, LACMA also opens its doors on various holidays like MLK Day, Columbus Day, and Labor Day. So you have no excuse to at least get a little culture in ya. LACMA.org

American Museum of Natural History – New York City: You probably already know about all the giant blue whale model and dinosaur bones in this extremely famous museum, but did you know that the entrance is a $16 suggested donation? Well it is... which means you can pay what you want. www.amnh.org/visitors/

St. Louis Science Center – St. Louis: It's always free at this hands-on science center. So if you're trying to figure why the hell gravity is keeping you from flying off the face of the earth, just come here. www.slsc.org

The Museum of Fine Arts – Boston: You could pretend to be interested in history at one of *those* museums, but why bother. Right? History's for nerds! Come here in on Wednesdays after 4:00pm when it's voluntary donation, and pay with your pocket lint. Even if they say otherwise, they actually like it. www.mfa.org/visit/admission

Learn to Cook

I know this goes without saying, but I'm gonna say it anyways. Learning to cook will save you lots of money. I only wish I took my own advice; I can't cook for shit. Besides all those reasons that I mentioned in the eating section, cooking your own food can save you money in the dating department too. Imagine there's some hottie you'd like to impress, but old Mister Jackson and his buddies Jefferson, Lincoln, and Washington have all taken a vacation from your wallet. Luckily since you stocked up at the store you've got some provisions for just this kind of situation. So instead of inviting your date to _____ (fill in with overpriced restaurant), you can say, "Hey, I don't know if you know this, but I make a killer _____ (fill this in with whatever dish you've mastered for this specific moment). Wanna come over and let me cook for you?" This my friend, combined with a bottle of wine or three (depending on how ugly you are), might just get you laid. BUT, and this is a big one, don't invite them over for your cooking on the first date. I'd say wait until at least the second one. Why? Well because inviting someone over for the first date just makes you seem a little shady. So this of course brings us to Cheap First Dates.

Cheap First Dates: If you're an idiot, then you think "expensive dinner" or some shit when you hear the words "first date". But don't worry, I'm gonna disabuse you of that notion (hey I've been verbally abusing you everywhere else). To begin with, the idea that spending a lot of money to impress someone completely goes against the Broke-Ass ethos. Look, you're broke, fuck it, who cares. If someone doesn't want to date you because of that, then you are way better off without them. They are resigned to a life of actually trying to keep up with the Kardashians. So with that in mind, if you do want to take someone out to dinner on a first date, be honest with yourself and take them to some place that's affordable. As I mentioned in the eating section, there's tons of good affordable places to eat out in every city. Just pick one and go there. Usually, the more unique the better. So if you know of a weird Japanese place with bondage porn on the walls that occasionally sells bull penis and gives you cotton candy for dessert (it's called Kenka and is in NYC), then take your date there...unless that's your mom's house.

In my dating life though, I've found that a straight-up dinner date is not really always the best move. Sure it gives you time to talk, but it lacks in creativity. Do something interesting. I've gone on ice cream dates, milkshake dates, skee-ball dates, coffee/tea dates, even just hanging out at the park dates. The more intriguing the invitation sounds (as long as it's not like "Wanna see my knife collection?"), the more interested the person will be in hanging out with you.

Personally, I've always been an advocate of drinking during dates. It allows for you to unwind a little easier, and let's face it–pants drop a little bit easier, too. For those of you who don't drink, (and for once I'm not judging you) a milkshake date is solid because, really, how much is a milkshake? Like $4 right? And if they're lactarded, cupcake dates are another quirky but cheap option.

If you do go for the boozy date, the best way to avoid paying for all the drinks is to order from the bar for each round and don't open a tab. When you order the night's first drink, your date will probably try to pay for his or her drink. To avoid any awkwardness while still avoiding paying for everything, say something like, "I got this round. You can get the next one if you want." It's the 21st century for fuck's sake, going Dutch is totally acceptable and if your date doesn't offer to pay for anything, then that's probably a sign you should watch out; anyone who's considering gold-digging your broke ass is probably totally detached from reality.

But out of all this I think the best way to get out of expensive first dates is the whole hanging out in a group thing. It worked in junior high, why can't it work now? The idea with this is simple, just be like, "Hey, some friends and I are gonna go watch this public decapitation that going on at in the town square. You and your friends should come along too." If there's a group of you, there's no pressure for you to pay for someone else's shit, yet the two of you can still talk to each other as much as you'd like while your friends occupy themselves or each other. And if you hit it off, you can always be like, "Wanna come over and let me cook you my amazing SpaghettiO's?"

Great Ideas for Creative Cheap Dates

Ice Cream or a Milkshake: Cheap, delicious and downright cute.... again, as long as nobody is lactose intolerant. I'll just leave it at that.

A Picnic: Hit up the store and get some sandwich fixins or some nibbles so that you have something to soak up that cheap wine you're bringing.

Go for a Walk or Hike: No matter where you live, there's gotta be somewhere that's at least *kinda* scenic. Even if you live in Fresno.

Take a Tour of A Brewery or Winery: You might end up paying an entrance fee, but at least the establishment is supplying the booze and giving you a little education behind it.

Go on a Scavenger Hunt: I don't personally have the motivation to organize something like this, but I've heard others do and actually have a lot of fun doing it. Good for you if you're one of them.

See a Game: Go on a discount day and get nosebleed seats. Sneak in a flask and some food so you don't end up buying the amazing smelling but overpriced garlic fries.

Bowling: Nothing says "sexy time" better than hanging out with fat rednecks rolling heavy balls down an alley.

Go to the County Fair: No matter where you are, this happens every summer and it's usually pretty cheap to get in, see some farm animals, ride a rickety rollercoaster, and eat some corn on the cob. By the way, have you ever noticed how carnies are pretty much land pirates? All kinds of eye patches and missing teeth and shit. If you haven't noticed it before, you will next time. In fact, I just gave you a great conversation topic for your date. You're welcome!

Art Openings: Free wine and cheese, and being able to feel classier than you really are.

Watch a Meteor Shower: These things happen multiple times a year. Find out when one is happening and drive out to some place where you can see the stars. You'll get to discover how many falling stars you have to wish upon in order for you to get laid. www.imo.net/calendar

Rent a Movie from the Library: They're free, plus you'll finally have an excuse to see an old classic like *Casablanca.*

See a High School Football Game: Just get *really* wasted and see how much screaming and belittling it takes before you get thrown out. You could make it a contest!

The Farmer's Market: Abundant free samples make it so nobody needs to spend any money.

Role Play: Decide on ridiculous characters and then go do something normal while acting like them, like a hipster or *Jersey Shore* cast member. This is your George Costanza moment: the weirder you act the more attractive you might seem.

Take a Tour of Your Favorite Neighborhood: Walking is free! Looking at things is free! Making up facts and stories to impress your date is free!

Teach Each Other a Hobby or Dish: You've both got to be good at something, right?

Play Board Games: See how sore of a loser the other person is early so you have time to bail.

Listening Party: Share your favorite albums with each other and talk about why you like them. Judge each other silently.

Play a Sport: Everyone was forced to take gym class at some point. Shoot some hoops or worst case, throw a Frisbee.

Fly A Kite: This is seriously effing adorable, and you'll make everyone else on a date who's not flying a kite feel like they're on the worst date ever.

Hang Out at an Empty Playground: Seriously, who doesn't love swinging? Make sure it's empty though to avoid concerned parents calling the cops on you–there's nothing sexy about being considered a child molester.

Fast Food Orgy: Drive around to a few different fast food places and get stuff off the $1 menu, then attack your heart attack picnic. This is probably why people in couples get fat.

Disposable Camera Day: Remember when you took pictures and had to actually wait to see what they looked like? It was actually pretty fun and you can get disposable cameras from the $1 store now. Walk around taking pictures then get them developed to see which of you was the asshole who had their finger on the lens the entire time.

Karaoke Night: Most bars don't charge for their karaoke nights, but you should probably pack a flask. You'll get wasted and do this together eventually, so why not as a date?

Broke-Ass Porn

Free Condoms

The old saying goes, "We all pay for sex somehow." Whether it's putting up with some fucking ego-centric blabbermouth just to get laid, or shelling out a week's salary to buy an overpriced dinner, you've gotta pay with either time or money. Plus you've also gotta pay for protection, because if you don't, you'll certainly pay for that later.

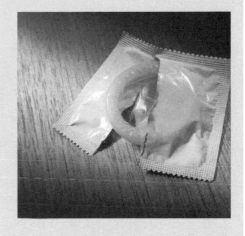

Luckily in most cities, there are plenty of places to get FREE condoms. In New York City, most bars have what looks like a tip jar full of prophylactics that you can pocket. It's not nearly as common in San Francisco to see the free rubbers in bars, but if you go out to any gay bar, free condoms are everywhere. And worse comes to worst, you can always go to Planned Parenthood or any other clinic. Their condoms may feel like having sex with sandpaper, but it's better than, you know, ruining the rest of your life with an STD.

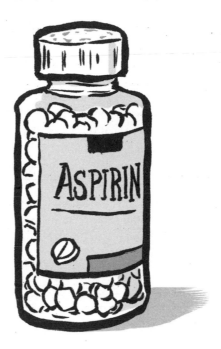

Mike Force

Health

If this chapter seems shorter than the rest, it's probably because it is. Truth be told, I'm just not a very healthy person. That being said, there's still plenty of good advice in here. Be sure to check out the stuff regarding insurance.

Planned Parenthood

There's nothing more expensive than having kids and nothing less sexy than having an infectious and deadly disease. Thankfully those conservative bastards haven't been able to shut Planned Parenthood down yet so us broke-asses are able to stay disease and baby free.

At the time I'm writing this (and knowing the complete absurdity of this country, I'm sure nothing has changed) there are still millions of Americans who can't afford health insurance. Whether you're looking for prenatal care, an abortion, an STD test, an HPV vaccine, birth control, condoms, the morning after pill, or you just wanna know why there's a weird weepy lesion on your dick, Planned Parenthood is there for you. And the best part is, their goal is to make it as affordable for you as possible!

Back in my younger, more promiscuous days, I used to visit Planned Parenthood every six months just to get tested for STDs. And the only problem I ever had there was running into someone I knew. Now that's awkward. It was like, "Soooo...what are you doing, er, I mean...how's English class?" But please, please don't ever let that stop you. It was only awkward because it was a girl a wanted to bang. Also, I advise against trying to pick up on someone in the Planned Parenthood waiting room. I'm just saying...

Go to PlannedParenthood.org to find a location near you.

Free Clinics

As I just mentioned, health insurance is really expensive in the US and since our country would rather spend money on wars than on the health and sanity of its citizens, a shit ton of you are uninsured. I'm sorry about that, because it seriously fucking sucks. Luckily though there are health havens in the form of free clinics, created specifically for people like us who enjoy what should be standard rights but somehow aren't.

You should know going in that free clinics will probably not be completely filled with attractive, cunning broke-asses such as yourself. There will also be people there who have serious problems, like homelessness, but also enjoy keeping their one life on earth as long as possible, too. And they may smell like urine. Also, since the clinics are almost always understaffed (or is it overpopular, hmm?), you will probably spend a fair amount of time in the waiting room. But the plus side is that it's free! So bring a nose plug and good book to read, and go get that weird looking tumor checked out. I had one that I named Guillermo that ended up being benign. Now I have a cool scar instead that I call "Guillermo's Grave." To find your nearest free clinic go to FreeClinics.us or FreeMedicalCamps.com.

Cheap Dentistry

Remember how I was just talking about free medical clinics (if not you should probably go visit one), well you can also get free dentistry at a lot of them as well. But just in case you make a smidgen over whatever the line is that separates low income people from those just above it, you should look into dentistry schools. Just like anything else, dentists need to practice so why not get your grill looked at by a student. The work they do is always supervised by a teacher and its way cheaper than going to a regular dentist. I mean, even if you have health insurance, how many people actually have dental insurance too? By the way, isn't that fucked up? Medical insurance doesn't cover your teeth or eyes?!? What the fuck? Yes another shake down by the insurance industry. I hope to god, satan and everything in between that those fuckers get their comeuppance soon and that it's brutal. The worst trick ever played on the American people is our current health care situation. OK, someone just grabbed the soapbox out from under me.

Discount Health Plans

Speaking of not having vision or dental coverage even if you are one of the lucky few of us with insurance, there are some discount plans out there that offer huge savings for a small membership fee, such as Careington (www.careington.com). Yes, they cost money to join but I know people who have saved hundreds through the discounts – just check to make sure they are accepted by your health care provider before signing up.

Cheap Shrinks

It's one thing when your friends describe you as, "Oh Jessica? She's so crazy. We had so much fun dancing on the bar the other night." It's another thing when your friends describe you as, "You know Jessica? That bitch is out of her goddamn mind! If she spent the night at my house I'd lock my bedroom door and sleep with a baseball bat." I'm not gonna lie, crazy people are pretty funny when they do weird shit in public and you can point and laugh and go on your way. That said, I've had some close friends lose their minds and it's a fucking scary thing to watch. Whether it's been drug induced psychosis or hereditary schizophrenia, I've seen some pretty lovely people end up in really dark places.

Luckily there affordable mental health options out there. The first thing you can do is contact the nearest university and see if they have psychology grad programs. Just like dentistry, often times grad students can offer some help. A good friend of mine did this and saw patients at the VA hospital while she was in school. You should also look into seeing if there are any mental health clinics in your area and then inquire about their pricing. Finally just ask Mr. Google, who you should have figured out is Best Bud Google by now. Use the search engine and type in "low cost health care" and the name of your town. Good luck, crazy pants.

Cheap Massages

When I get a massage I like someone to pretty much beat the shit out of my back. As far as I'm concerned you can drop a Jimmy "Superfly" Snuka flying elbow onto me. That being said, beggars can't be choosers and I can rarely a good massage, but fortunately we have massage schools. People gotta train somewhere right? Since these folks are students who need a certain amount of hours practice to become certified, you can get really cheap deals. Just contact the massage schools near you to see what kind of deals they're offering.

The same thing applies for acupuncture, but it's up to you to decide whether you want to trust a novice with sticking big ass needles into you.

Cheap Eyeglasses

I've been blessed with super good eyesight. I've never worn glasses or contacts, although I feel like staring into this damn computer everyday is starting to send me in that direction. Those of you who do have bad eyeballs and need prescription lenses know how expensive it can be. Luckily for you, my friend Ebony told me about this website called ZenniOptical.com. Zenni Optical has literally over 5,000 different kinds stylish glasses (lenses included) starting at only $8 and maxing out at around $30! Crazy right? Aren't glasses normally like $200 or some ridiculous number like that? Here's the catch though: I'm pretty sure the glasses are made in sweatshops in China. I'll leave the rest up to you, your eyeballs, and your conscience.

Insurance

Fuck, where do I begin on this one? The situation is fucked and there really is no such thing as cheap insurance. There's "cheaper" insurance, but it's still expensive. That being said, the Jewish mother in me really wants you to have some. What can I say? I worry about you all.

Since I'm really no expert on this whole thing I decided to talk to someone who is. I first heard about Alex Maiolo while reading *Spin Magazine.* Journalist David Peisner did a story in the December '09 issue about the American Health care system and how it affects musicians. I'll paraphrase it and tell you the answer: it treats them poorly. Anyways, Alex was quoted at length in the article, so I contact David and he hooked me up with Alex.

In Yiddish, Alex Maiolo would be called a *mensch,* aka a good person. While his regular job is as an agent for property and casualty insurance, he also volunteers his time, offering free advice to struggling artists and musicians trying to navigate through the twisted and confusing American health care system. Alex and Future of Music (FutureOfMusic.org) created Health Insurance Navigation Tool (HINT) which provides "informed, musician-friendly support and advice to musicians who need information about health insurance, for free." You can check them out at FutureOfMusic.org/issues/campaigns/get-hint. Technically you're supposed to be a musician for HINT to be able to help you out, but you are one right (wink, wink, nudge nudge)? Luckily for all of us, Alex was nice enough to lay some info for me, so here we go:

Part of the reason insurance is so damn complicated is that each state has different laws regarding it. Your rights versus the insurance companies' rights differ state to state. Some states regulate with the consumer in mind while others do the opposite. So to see what the laws are in your state and how they apply to you, go to the Artists' Health Insurance Resource Center (ahirc.org). The AHIRC is, "an up-to-date, comprehensive and unbiased database of health care resources for artists, performers, freelancers and the self-employed." At the time I'm writing this, the Obama administration is putting the finishing touches on their health insurance overhaul. The AHIRC will be the place to keep you updated on how the changes affect you individually. They do not, however, sell you insurance or tell you from which outfit to buy.

If you don't have health insurance, Alex has three suggestions for getting some:

1. Get short term insurance: If you're healthy you can buy chunks of insurance for 6 months or a year at a time. The problem with this is that each time you renew your insurance, either after the 6 months or 12 months, the companies have the opportunity to choose not to renew you. Also only some states allow you to take this route, New York and Vermont aren't one of them. This insurance is best for people who are young and healthy because they are less likely to come down with something that requires long term coverage. Usually when you're all young and virile, the only things that land you giant hospital bills are your own stupidity, poor decisions, and bad luck. Alex likes to think of these policies as a cheap but not perfect way to manage catastrophic losses.

2. Get a job with benefits for people working 30 hours a week or more: Look I get it, you're working part time so you can do school, or be in a band, or write books or whatever. But how much are you currently working? What's another five or six hours a week if it will get you health insurance benefits. Ask your boss if you can bump up your hours so you can get in on their health insurance plan. If your place of employment doesn't offer it, try getting a gig with a big, worker friendly corporation like Whole Foods, Starbucks or Trader Joe's. Sure "working for the man" isn't all that cool, but having health insurance is, especially if you're still only working part time and able to have your freedom, too. Apparently Starbucks gives insurance to people who work only something like 20 hours a week! And you might even learn how to say the names of their drinks without sounding like someone who doesn't know how to read. (Or is that just me?)

3. Buy your own insurance policy: This can be expensive or inexpensive depending on many things, which is where I'm going now:

If you're gonna buy your own insurance policy you have to think about what you're trying to accomplish. How often do you go to the doctor? How often do you need prescriptions? Generally speaking, if you're young and healthy, you're not doing either of these very often. What you need is insurance that covers you if some kind of major emergency happens, like getting hit by a car or falling off a roof. Sure it would be nice to have the insurance company pick up the tab for your pills and visits, but that's gonna cost you more per month. If you only see the doc once or twice a year, it's gonna be cheaper if you just pay for those things yourself instead of paying a higher fee each month. You feel me?

If you're young, healthy and broke here's what you should do:

Get a plan that has a high deductible but low monthly payments. Think about it like this: lets say you're riding your bike and a driver hits you and takes off and isn't found. If you have no insurance you can be on the line for hundreds of thousands of dollars in hospital bills. No matter how good you are at fundraising, are you gonna be able to get together $500,000 to pay for that shit? Hell no!

Imagine the same thing happens but you have a plan with a deductible of $5,000. While you'll have to pay every penny of that $5,000 afterwards, you won't have to pay all that much more. In the occasion of a catastrophe, you pay your deductible, then you and the insurance split the costs up to a certain amount (this is called co-insurance) and after that, the insurance company picks up the rest of the tab. While having to come up with $7,000 or $10,000 is a motherfucking bitch, it's totally possible. You're young, you're cool (I mean anyone who buys this book *must* be), you know people in bands. Throwing a fundraiser or two will help you pay off those hospital bills in no time. But unless you get Kings of Leon to play, coming up with $500,000 for hospital bills is damn near impossible.

Exercising on the Cheap

While people exercise for different reasons, I put this in the Health section instead of the Beauty one because I'm part of the segment of America that likes to lie to itself. We tell ourselves that we exercise for the health benefits, but the truth is we just do it so that people will continue to be interested in having sex with us. Then again I also just lied to you: I don't really work out at all.

Yoga by Donation: My last experience with yoga was in San Francisco where I did a free trial session at a place that turned the room temp to 105° (and the humidity to 40%). They call this style Bikram Yoga, but I call it smelling like funky-ass feet. I couldn't handle the heat/stench/muscle pains so I left halfway through the session (go ahead call me a pussy. I know you're gonna do it anyway.). But lately I've considered trying yoga again and if I were to do it, it would of course be at yoga by donation.

In San Francisco and New York there are multiple place that do yoga by donation. I also know that there are other cities like Tucson, Arizona and Portsmouth, New Hampshire that have studios that run on a similar principal. To find out if there's one near you google "yoga by donation" and the name of your town.

Alternatively if you wanna do yoga from the comfort of your own home (naked yoga anyone?) you should go to the YogaToThePeople. com and click on "Try a Class Online". YTTP started off doing yoga by donation in NY's East Village and has now expanded to SF, Berkeley, and Seattle. These cats want you to get your downward dog on so badly that they have nine free classes online. Now you have no excuse for not having an awesome yoga butt. Well actually, laziness is still a good excuse as far as I'm concerned.

Cheap Gyms: I heard somewhere that the legendary running back, Ricky Watters, never went to the gym. Each day he just did thousands of sit ups, push ups and whatever other kind of ups that people do. Personally, that sounds horrible to me, but that's just because I hate working out. For those of you who want to get bigger and stronger and not have to spend half your day at it, there are these things called gyms. I've been to one before.

A lot of gyms give you deals where you just pay like $25 bucks a month. That's not too bad considering that this generally includes all kinds of classes you can take too. But if $25 a month is too much I recommend checking out your nearest community rec center. Many of them have work out equipment and often times it's either free or a very small fee paid once a year. Also check out your local YMCA. They can be cheaper than gyms, but sometimes have less workout equipment and very few amenities. Then again when was the last time you could afford *any* amenities?

Another thing you can do is sign up for the free trial memberships that the gyms give out. These are often good for a couple weeks, and depending on how many gyms are in your town, you can probably get a few months of working our for free if you just keep "trying out" new places.

Play a Sport: Over the past few years I've been seeing shit like kickball leagues popping up in different cities throughout the US. While the games often include drinking of some sort, playing kickball is still technically exercise. Why not have fun while you exercise right? Get a pick up game of basketball going or maybe join a softball league. I've also seen some dodgeball happening at Dolores Park in San Francisco recently. Who doesn't like dodgeball? Worse comes to worse you can always start your own league using craigslist of facebook. Ah, the beauty of the Internet, bringing people together for strange and often unwholesome activities.

Ride a Bike: I'm pretty sure I covered this back in the Traveling chapter (p.47), but riding a bike kills all kinds of birds with one stone. Not only does it keep you fit, it also saves you money in the whole getting from point A to point B realm. And it leaves no carbon footprint at all. That's like a trifecta of awesomeness, as opposed to the trifecta of sadness when I picked the wrong horses at the track the other day.

Go Jogging: Ugh, I hate jogging. But it's definitely one of the most free forms of exercise you can do.

Download Workout Videos: Fuck paying for workout videos, just download them. They've been making these things since the invention of the VCR, so there are thousands out there for consumption. Watch a few to see which is the absolute least annoying, and then work that *tuchus* of yours. If you don't know what a tuchus is, you need more Jewish friends.

Also just google "free workout videos" or "free work out routines" to get a whole assortment of different websites to choose from.

Babysitting: Laura Smith, NYC editor for BrokeAssStuart.com, has some good insight into this one:

You ever feel sore in muscles you never use and can't figure out why?

Riding back to New York after the holidays, I couldn't figure out why my arms were so sore. I didn't do any fist pumping or chopping wood, or god forbid actual push-ups, then I figured it out. I was lifting kids most of the time. Have you ever SEEN a parent's arms, those things are like tree trunks. So I figure why not get paid and get free exercise in the process while babysitting. Sometimes they even run and you have to catch them. Free cardio! Register at SitterCity.com and receive job alerts for sitter opportunities all over the city. I'm not talking about signing your life over to nannydom, but if you're ever strapped for cash, think about those jiggle-free arms you had at the tender age of 15, right at the peak of your babysitting days.

Getting Laid: I mean it's not like I need to try to convince you have more sex, I'm but I'm just saying, having sex burns calories and gets your heart rate up. Unless you have sex with me of course; I'll give you the best 30 seconds of your life. 45 if I'm drunk.

Mike Force

Beauty

The number one way to save on beauty products? Befriend someone who works in the beauty industry and make them give you free samples, of course! If that doesn't work or more likely, that friend gets tired of giving you free shit all the time for nothing in return, I've put together some suggestions that are (and will keep you) very doable.

Befriend The Dollar Store

I talk about this in the "Shopping" chapter also but Dollar/99 Cent stores are a broke-ass's BFF. For some reason—maybe because it's stuff we grew up just always having around without ever thinking about how it cost your parents money to get there—things like soap, shampoo, conditioner, toothpaste, deodorant and other items roommates and fellow office mates hope we use are annoying as shit to pay for. But the Dollar Store says, "Hey. I don't get why the fuck shampoo is $5.99 at the drug store either, especially since you can't really tell the difference between using that and dish soap. How about I do you a solid and give you this bottle of shampoo here for just $1." And then you say thank you and so does your girlfriend/boyfriend, and then you put the dish soap back in the kitchen before your roommate notices it's gone.

Rewards Card and Coupons

Definitely join your local drug store's rewards program and go through the ads each week to see what's on sale (or go online, almost all post them now!). Coolsavings.com and SmartSource.com are a couple sites awesome for finding and printing coupons to save even more money.

Dude Looks Like A Lady

Products like razors and shaving cream are hands down cheaper for men than women. So ladies, your razor won't be pink and your legs won't smell like "Kiwi Sprinkles of Sunset Magic" or whatever, but you will save yourself some serious cash.

Look Around Your House

Guess what? A lot of the stuff you already have lying around can be used for keeping yourself layable, so no excuses! Here are some suggestions...

Lemon: Mix 1/4 cup lemon juice and 3/4 cup water and spray onto your hair for natural highlights that will hopefully be nothing like the polka-dot experience you had with Sun-In back in middle school. Swish some fresh juice for fresh breath. Rub fresh lemon on dark/rough spots like elbows and knees (I'm not asking how you got them, I'm just suggesting a solution).

Cucumber: Slices of 'cuke are great for de-poofing eyes, and you can snack on them after.

Milk: The lactic acid in milk serves as an exfoliant and its fat content acts as a moisturizer. Add a gallon of whole milk to a tubful of warm water and soak. Apologize to your roommates for using all of their milk because you thought it'd be cool to take a bath in it. Milk is also good for soothing irritated skin after sunburn or (gulp) waxing.

Green Tea: Make some green tea, let it cool down, and splash those antioxidants all up over your grill. Then, place the steeped tea bags over your eyes to reduce swelling from playing *Call of Duty* until 5AM.

Eggs: Use egg whites for a 5-minute face mask. Use egg yolks for an omelet to enjoy while you're waiting to take off your face mask.

Honey: If you've got frizzy hair, use honey instead of buying expensive anti-frizz products. After shampooing your hair, massage a tablespoon of honey into damp hair. Wait 5 minutes and then rinse well with warm water.

Sugar: Mix brown sugar with some honey or olive oil and rub all over your hands for easy exfoliation. Yes, it is OK to lick your fingers after.

Salt: Mix several tablespoons of sea salt with water and put it in a spray bottle. Spray on your hair next time you want to lie about having gone on a beach vacation.

Oatmeal: This keeps things moving right along in or out of the body so mix with milk powder and honey for a facial cleanser that will get rid of breakouts. Oatmeal baths have also been a remedy for chicken pox or poison ivy for years, just put some in a cheesecloth and throw it in the tub with some milk.

Olive Oil: Got dry skin/lips/hair? Lube yourself up with some EVOO. It also works great as a shaving cream and as a makeup remover—and you will taste extremely delicious.

Baby Powder: Best way ever to cover up the fact you were too hungover to shower? Baby powder. Just sprinkle a little on your finger tips and massage into the roots of your hair to instantly erase your night out.

Baking Soda: This little fella can do just about anything with a little water. Add a splash of water and dab on zits. Mix with water, a little salt and use as toothpaste. Mix with just water and use as mouthwash, and heal mouth sores.

Aloe Plant: Best way to make the sunburn you got when you passed out after your ill-fated Margarita Morning idea feel better. Also awesome for clearing up the aftermath of pimples.

Aspirin: Crush two or three aspirins and add them to your shampoo if you want to fight dandruff. It works because aspirin contains salicylic acid, which is the same ingredient used in dandruff fighting shampoo.

Beer: I know, I know—this better be worth wasting a good beer. Apparently, the vitamin B, sugars, and acidity of the beer help remove built-up product residue and give tons of shine. So shampoo and rinse as normal and then do a waterfall over your head and hope for the best. Yeastier the better, so go for a Guinness. Needless to say, you should rinse thoroughly after to avoid keghead.

Your Bed: Put a pile of books under your headboard so it's raised six inches. Sleep for two hours. Awake looking like you slept for eight hours.

Vaseline: Speaking of your bedroom... Actually, petroleum jelly is like a secret beauty black ninja. It's awesome as a hair product, lip gloss, stain remover, moisturizer, natural mascara and more.

Toothpaste: Why spend tons of money on zit cream when you brush your teeth with it everyday? If you feel a zit coming on, put a dab of toothpaste on it before you go to bed. Do this two nights in a row, and that red bastard will never break the surface.

What are some of YOUR secret tips? Email me at info@ brokeassstuart.com

And here are some not so normal uses for not so normal products...

- Preparation H for under-eye bags
- Monistat Anti-Chafing Powder Gel as a makeup primer (um, your call on this one...)
- Chapstick to smooth out eyebrows
- Deodorant on smelly feet
- Use Johnson's Baby Shampoo No More Tears formula as a makeup remover

For Girls Who Gussy Up

Pick Your Best (or Worst) Feature & Focus on It:

If you've got great eyes, invest in products to play them up and leave the rest of your face/lips close to bare. If you have bad skin, spend your money on quality skin care instead of bright green eye liner. Or, go for red lipstick and keep the rest of your face simple. It's a classic for a reason and seems to have the magical ability to turn even the most busted girls into babes.

Buy Products with Many Functions:

Companies are getting hip to how lazy you are so tons of products are made for multiple uses now, like lip stains that can also be used on cheeks and eyes (well, eyelids). Even if they're not specifically marketed that way, doesn't hurt to try it out on your own. If you're like most girls, you probably have extra products you don't use anymore so why not see if you like that bright pink blush you bought for an 80s party better as an eye shadow?

Spa at Home

So, this stuff is strictly for the ladies (and boys who like to dress up like ladies)...

Get Hot and Steamy:

Bathrooms are pretty disgusting. Before doing this, you should decide if yours is a place you actually want to be uncomfortably hot in for an extended amount of time.

Homemade Sauna

• Bring a cold bowl or spray bottle of water with ice cubes into the bathroom.

• Use towels to block the crack under your bathroom door.

Run the hottest water possible in the shower and sink. Point the showerhead toward the wall so you don't accidentally get splashed, and pull back the shower curtain. Turn off the water once you feel it's hot enough.

• Make sure you locked the damn door.

• Get naked and close your eyes. Pretend you are anywhere but in your gross bathroom.

Skin Moisturizing Treatment

Question: "How do you warm up lotion?" Answer: "Masturbate with it." Or, you can just put your body lotion on top of your radiator while you shower.

Deep Conditioning Hair Treatment:

Work your regular conditioner through damp hair, then put on a shower cap and blast your head for a few minutes under your hairdryer on low. Rinse well and then go buy yourself a beer with the money you just saved.

DIY Mani/Pedi:

Buying all the crap for a manicure and pedicure can add up really quickly. Here's a way to use some of the stuff you already have around for a polished nail look that won't chip every time you get into a bar fight.

Supplies (grab anything you don't have from the $1 Store):

• Small nail scissors
• Whole milk
• Baking Soda
• Olive Oil
• Angled nail stick
• Nail file
• Buffing block

For Manicure:

1) Soak hands in a bowl of warm whole milk for 3-5 minutes.

For Pedicure:

1) Add 4 Tbs. of baking soda to a quart of warm water and soak your feet for 10 minutes.

2) Use nail scissors to cut up any little snags of skin around your nails.

3) Push back cuticles with an angled-nail stick.

4) File nails into a rounded square shape.

5) Use a nail buffer to buff the surface of nails.

6) Warm olive oil and rub into your hands and cuticles.

7) Go grab some asses with your pretty new paws!

Get Yer Hair Did

Free Haircuts: If you can't afford an expensive ass haircut, you can always go to one of the salon schools, and get your hair cut for super cheap or free. The downside to this is that these haircuts can take up to a couple hours because there is generally an instructor there walking the student through. But you basically aren't paying shit for the haircut, so who gives a fuck. The people cutting your hair are the same ones that will be charging like $100 a haircut some time in the near future, so this is a pretty killer deal. To find the nearest one to you just Google "salon school" and the name of your town (or nearest big city). Then call the salon and see what you can work out. A lot of times the salon will offer other extremely discounted services like facials or colorings too.

Get a Bang Trim: The funny thing about this title is that guys and girls probably read it two different ways. The girls read it as it actually is, and the guys read it as "Get to Bang Trim." Sorry fellas this is about haircuts, you might want skip to the next thing on here. Anyways, if you've got a hair style that you're sticking with, like having bangs, most hair stylists will let you come in between appointments for a quick touch up. Since you're just getting a little maintenance and not getting anything new done, it won't take your stylist very long. Just make sure you get it done by the same person who actually cut your hair in the first place. It's all about loyalty with these people.

Cut your Own Hair: I have unsteady hands, poor coordination and bad aim, but I've cut my hair own before. Actually let me rephrase that: I've shaved my own head before. Buying a $20 pair of clippers is a great investment because you can just shave your head anytime you need a haircut, and then have a friend touch up the spots you missed. It saves you a ton of money.

The only time this backfired for me was the time my clippers broke part way through giving myself a trim. I was living in a Puerto Rican part of Brooklyn at the time and since my hair looked so fucked up, I had to go to the corner barber to have him finish the job. I told him to shave it on the 3 setting which he did, but then he squared up my forehead and made my sideburns come down into points like icicles. When I got home I introduced my girlfriend to her new Puerto Rican Jewish boyfriend.

If you're not looking to shave your head, you can still cut your own hair. If you're not going for anything too crazy like different layers or Farrah Fawcett hair (or anything stylish at all actually), you can pretty much just give yourself a trim with scissors and then have a friend clean it up for you. Or so I'm told. I've not actually done this myself because I am definitely not skilled enough even for a basic attempt. Out of all the homemade haircut situations though, the best I ever had was when I was in college. Back then I had short spiky hair that was dyed a bright fire engine red. I also had this female friend who would come over to my house, cut, bleach and dye my hair for me, for free, and then we'd hook up. To say it was an awesome deal is an understatement. Maybe you can find one for yourself.

Crafty DIY Bath & Beauty Products

By Kate Kotler (KateKotler.com)

I don't know about you, but I could easily – EASILY – spend a $100 per visit in the bath and beauty sections of Whole Foods or any other crunchy and organic store snapping up yummy, smell good products to use in the bathroom.

How to:

Place the glass measuring cup into the pot (filled with water) and place it on the stove. When the water is boiling place all ingredients into the measuring cup and continue to simmer until they melt. Give the mixture a good stir, combining the ingredients well. Pour them into the pretty jar and add 10-20 drops of your essential oil. Close the jar tightly and put into the fridge for a couple of hours to solidify the mixture. Take it out and store it at room temp for use. You will use your fingers to scoop out a small amount to spread onto your wet armpits after a shower and the jar should last you for two to three months, at least, depending on how stinky you actually are.

Lavender Sugar Shower Scrub:

What you need...

- One cup of raw sugar
- One ounce of sweet almond oil
- One Vitamin E gel cap (puncture the cap and squeeze the oil out)
- One tablespoon of unrefined cocoa butter
- 6-10 drops of essential oil
- A large glass mixing bowl
- A pretty jar with a lid that screws on

How to:

In the large glass mixing bowl combine the raw sugar and almond oil. Once it is well combined add in the Vitamin E, the cocoa butter and your essential oil. Mix well and place into the jar, making sure to cover it tightly. You can add more or less almond oil and cocoa butter as desired if you have really dry skin or would prefer a dry scrub mix. Use a shower puff or sponge with the scrub for the best results.

Happy-Peppy Hand Sanitizer:

What you need...

- One cup of rubbing alcohol
- One ounce of tea tree oil
- Two Vitamin E gel caps (puncture caps and squeeze out the oil)
- 20 drops of lavender or rose essential oil
- A small spray bottle

———

It is one of my few my girly trappings. I love scented soaps, scrubs, oils and all products to make you softer, scentier and more sensual. I suspect I am not the only one with this affliction or the only one who has had their personal budget suffer on a monthly basis due to what I like to call "excess product spending."

The thing is that you can totally make these products yourself with very little effort for half to two thirds the total price on what you'd spend on a pre-packaged product... Not only is it cost-efficient to do this, but it is sustainable, as well, due to the fact that you're making in bulk AND reusing containers AND eliminating manufacturing costs. That is a eco-friendly win-win-win!

Plus, if you're creative about the packaging – using antique bottles and handcrafted labels and pretty ribbons and such – these homemade products make great gifts. (Or, creative things to sell in an Etsy shop to make a little extra cash.)

The only requirement is that in any of these recipes you not use patchouli oil as your essential oil, EVER. Seriously we don't need more dirty hippy smell in the world! I will personally hunt you down and smack your ass up with a yardstick like a crazed DIY nun if I hear of anyone making any of these using patchouli. For realzies.

Here are four recipes for DIY bath & beauty products that are sure to please:

DIY Deodorant:

What you need...

- A quart glass measuring cup
- A two quart pot
- Three tablespoons of unrefined shea butter
- Three tablespoons of baking powder
- Two tablespoons of arrowroot powder
- Two tablespoons of unrefined cocoa butter
- Two Vitamin E gel caps (puncture the caps and squeeze the oil out)
- 10-20 drops of your favorite essential oil
- A pretty 1/4 pint jar

How to:

Place the glass measuring cup into the pot (filled with water) and place it on the stove. When the water is boiling place all ingredients into the measuring cup and continue to simmer until they melt. Give the mixture a good stir, combining the ingredients well. Pour them into the pretty jar and add 10-20 drops of your essential oil. Close the jar tightly and put into the fridge for a couple of hours to solidify the mixture. Take it out and store it at room temp for use. You will use your fingers to scoop out a small amount to spread onto your wet armpits after a shower and the jar should last you for two to three months, at least, depending on how stinky you actually are.

Lavender Sugar Shower Scrub:

What you need...

- One cup of raw sugar
- One ounce of sweet almond oil
- One Vitamin E gel cap (puncture the cap and squeeze the oil out)
- One tablespoon of unrefined cocoa butter
- 6-10 drops of essential oil
- A large glass mixing bowl
- A pretty jar with a lid that screws on

How to:

In the large glass mixing bowl combine the raw sugar and almond oil. Once it is well combined add in the Vitamin E, the cocoa butter and your essential oil. Mix well and place into the jar, making sure to cover it tightly. You can add more or less almond oil and cocoa butter as desired if you have really dry skin or would prefer a dry scrub mix. Use a shower puff or sponge with the scrub for the best results.

Happy-Peppy Hand Sanitizer:

What you need...

- One cup of rubbing alcohol
- One ounce of tea tree oil
- Two Vitamin E gel caps (puncture caps and squeeze out the oil)
- 20 drops of lavender or rose essential oil
- A small spray bottle

——

It is one of my few my girly trappings. I love scented soaps, scrubs, oils and all products to make you softer, scentier and more sensual. I suspect I am not the only one with this affliction or the only one who has had their personal budget suffer on a monthly basis due to what I like to call "excess product spending."

The thing is that you can totally make these products yourself with very little effort for half to two thirds the total price on what you'd spend on a pre-packaged product... Not only is it cost-efficient to do this, but it is sustainable, as well, due to the fact that you're making in bulk AND reusing containers AND eliminating manufacturing costs. That is a eco-friendly win-win-win!

Plus, if you're creative about the packaging – using antique bottles and handcrafted labels and pretty ribbons and such – these homemade products make great gifts. (Or, creative things to sell in an Etsy shop to make a little extra cash.)

The only requirement is that in any of these recipes you not use patchouli oil as your essential oil, EVER. Seriously we don't need more dirty hippy smell in the world! I will personally hunt you down and smack your ass up with a yardstick like a crazed DIY nun if I hear of anyone making any of these using patchouli. For realzies.

Here are four recipes for DIY bath & beauty products that are sure to please:

DIY Deodorant:

What you need...

- A quart glass measuring cup
- A two quart pot
- Three tablespoons of unrefined shea butter
- Three tablespoons of baking powder
- Two tablespoons of arrowroot powder
- Two tablespoons of unrefined cocoa butter
- Two Vitamin E gel caps (puncture the caps and squeeze the oil out)
- 10-20 drops of your favorite essential oil
- A pretty 1/4 pint jar

How to:

Combine the alcohol, tea tree oil, lavender or rose essential oil and Vitamin E in the spray bottle. Close tightly and shake to combine the ingredients. You will want to shake the bottle each time before use. Tea Tree Facial Toner:

What you need...

- A large cosmetic squeeze or spray bottle (16 oz)
- 16 ounces of Witch Hazel
- Four ounces of tea tree oil

How to:

Combine ingredients in the bottle and shake well. Apply to your face using a cotton pad or ball. Can also be used to take the sting or itch away from mosquito bites, bee stings and small scrapes or cuts.

Financial Stuff

Consider this chapter broken up into three parts. The first part is just general shit I've come across in my years of brokeitude that has kept me afloat. For the second part, called "Actual Financial Coaching for Your Broke Ass," I consulted with Betsy Crouch (coachsizzle.com). She wrote the financial section for brokeassstuart.com for quite some time and is a professional financial coach (meaning she knows what the hell she's talking about). The third part is some interesting (OK, not really) financial shit you should know so that you can grow the fuck up and make responsible decisions about your finances.

Part 1: General Shit That Has Kept Me Afloat

Live without the shit you don't need.. One of the of the easiest ways to save money is also the most annoying: simplifying your life. There are so many little expenditures that all of us have that, when minimized, can save tons of money. For many of us, they are quality-of-life things. Think about it, do you really need your coffee to be from Starbucks? Fuck no, you can just brew some at home. What about that Twix bar that you have a few times a week? Sure, all that chocolate and caramel might be delicious, but it's not that necessary, is it? Take a week and write down *every single thing* you spend money on. This means all your bills—even your credit card payments and magazine subscriptions. At the end of the week look over the list and see which things are essential and which you can do without. Then start cutting some of the unneeded crap from your life. I told you it was annoying.

Get unemployment benefits. The first thing you need to do in order to receive unemployment is get laid off by no fault of your own. That part that I emboldened (ooh, you like it when I conjugate like that, don't you?) is important. If you get fired for walking into your terrible boss's office and taking a shit on her carpet, you will not be able to receive unemployment. You will just be awesome.

If you get let go from your job, you need to apply for your unemployment benefits. In many states you can just do it online by following the directions on your state's unemployment office website. In some states, you will have to go down to the office and apply in person. Like everything in this country, rules and regulations vary from state to state, so all the specifics of how much they pay you and what you must do to continue receiving benefits varies. Generally speaking, though, you'll be making about half (or less) of what you were previously making at your job. File for unemployment as soon as you stop working. In this fucked-up economic situation we're in, you never know how long it will take to find a new gig.

Get back money that you're owed. OK, I know this sounds like total bullshit, but there could actually be some money floating around out there that's owed to you. I first heard about this concept from a zine called Street Worthy Zine (streetworthyzine.com), but then just the other day, Andrew Dalton (dolfapedia.org) posted about it on brokeassstuart.com. To quote Andrew:

> I worked at a Best Buy in college for a whopping three weeks
> before peacing out because they "lost" my time-off request

and wanted me to come in to work at 4 a.m. the day after Thanksgiving and stand there for 12 hours ringing up rednecks with $25 DVD players while Maroon 5 played on a 30-minute loop over the loudspeakers. Obviously, I didn't make it back after the turkey coma. But it turns out they still owed me some minor portion of a paycheck, which I didn't know about until a couple weeks ago—about 6 years after the fact.

Apparently, all Andrew had to do was go to missingmoney.com, follow directions, and claim his money. While he was unfortunately only owed $35, think about how many bottles of Tapatio he can buy with that! Unclaimed.org is another website that does the same thing. If you don't find anything on those sites, Google the name of your state and "unclaimed property" and you will be lead to a database that might have info on some of your loot. Try this for every state you've lived in. And if you somehow get a ton of money, send me a little. Purty please?

Get a lawyer. Yes, seriously. If you're in the arts long enough, and you're actually good at whatever the fuck you're doing, chances are you're eventually gonna come across someone wanting you to sign a contract. Let me tell you this in bold, capital letters so it seems like I'm screaming it at you: DON'T SIGN ANYTHING WITHOUT HAVING A LAWYER LOOK IT OVER!!! There are shady people out there who will fuck you over and take you for all you're worth–even all your future earnings, too. Yeah, shitty, right?
I know right now you're like, "Come on, *dooood*, I can't afford a stinkin' lawyer. You're a dick for yelling at me like that." Well, I've got news for you, kiddo, you *can* afford a lawyer–kinda. Scattered throughout the country there are Lawyers for the Arts organizations. Basically these orgs hook you up with attorneys who are willing to do deeply discounted and even pro bono work for artists who qualify, and I'm pretty sure being a broke-ass is one of the qualifications. There's a Lawyers for the Arts organization in at least 30 states.

Go to court. A good friend of mine was wasted while walking home from the bar one night and decided to take a piss on the police station. It was certainly not one of his brightest moments, especially when the person who had been watching the security cameras came out and gave him a ticket. I can just imagine the person giving my boy a look like, "You've gotta be one of the dumbest motherfuckers I've seen in a long time." Anyway, he decided to challenge the ticket to see if they would reduce the fine. When he showed up to court, the cop who issued the ticket didn't, so the ticket was thrown out and my buddy didn't have to pay it. The moral of the story is that, in bigger cities, cops have better things to do than appear in court for petty shit. If you get written up for something minor, challenge it! You could very well get off without having to pay a fine.

Ask for reduced rates on your utilities. There's a great book called *Time Off!: The Upside of Downtime*, by Kristine Enea and Dean LaTourrette, which is pretty much a guide for people who've decided to take some time off work, whether it be a sabbatical or that thing people are now calling "funemployment" (I always just thought it was called getting shit-canned). Anyway, while researching this fine and masterful book that you're now holding, I picked up *Time Off* and learned this: If you're considered low-income you can get reduced rates on utilities like phone, gas, garbage and water. Awesome, right? You'll have to do some research to find out if you qualify as "low income" but shit, it can't hurt to ask right? One thing *Time Off* notes, though, is, "If you qualify at the beginning of the year but end up earning more than the income cut-off, you'll owe the difference between the regular rate and what you already paid."

Get a Salvation Army utility grant. This is another one I got from *Time Off*. The Salvation Army (salvationarmyusa.org) isn't just a place to get $2 tee shirts and mismatched furniture. Believe it or not, it's primarily an organization that's been helping poor people get by for nearly 150 years. While they do thousands of good things for poor people on a daily basis, something that's not often discussed is that they will give you a one-time grant to help you pay your utility bills. Call 1-800-933-9677 and ask about the REACH program: Relief for Energy Assistance through Community Help.

Find out about other grants. If you're in a really hard situation and need some serious help, I recommend researching drop-in centers and social services in your town. Ten minutes of Google research will help you find someone who might have some answers for you. For example, Chicago, San Francisco, and New York all have organizations that provide a one-time grant to help you pay your rent. While some of these programs are funded by the state or city, many of them are paid for by private or religious organizations. Your best bet is to connect with a social worker and talk through all the options.

Things To Do When You're Really Poor

There's a difference between being broke and being poor. Being poor is a socioeconomic thing; it's about not succeeding in a system designed to keep you down. Most people who are poor have either been born into it, or have made bad decisions (or had some made for them) that have put them in that situation. In a nation as rich as ours, the fact that poverty exists is truly a crime.

Being broke, on the other hand, is more of a temporary thing. People who are broke generally won't be so forever. Many people choose to be broke, sacrificing comfort and stability to chase the things that they desire—music, art, travel, whatever. The following is a list of things to you can do to help to immediately cut some costs if you find yourself sliding into the category of being poor. I've touched on a lot of this in various chapters of this book, so consider this a cheat-sheet.

Drop your landline and prepay a mobile. Landlines and cell phone plans cost a flat monthly rate no matter how much you use them. Getting a prepaid phone lets you use exactly as much time as you need without paying extra. You can then add more time when you see fit. Try to text instead of talk because you are charged per text instead of per minute. Also, use pay phones when you can, since they cost a lot less than cellular minutes. While pay phones are rare these days, you can still find them at places like shopping malls, bus depots, train stations, gas stations, and chain restaurants.

You can also use Gmail to make free calls across the U.S. In your Google Chat list, the top friend, "call phone," will be your broke ass's best freaking buddy. This is also extremely handy in case of a lost cell phone.

Don't sell your computer. If you have to start selling and pawning stuff, make sure to hold onto your computer, especially if it's a laptop. In case you haven't figured it out from all the urls listed in this book, the Internet is pretty much the best way to access any information. While you might be able to get a few hundred bucks for your computer, it's worth so much more to you if you keep it. It'll be what connects you to jobs, housing, and more. If you have a wireless card, don't pay for Internet, just go to a café or a public wireless hotspot place. If you do have to pay for Internet at home, look into a cheap dial-up service. They're usually only $10 a month. **If you don't have a computer:** Not having a computer can be a hassle, but there are plenty of public places where you can access the Internet. Public libraries, universities, and community colleges generally have computer labs that can be used for free. Also, try going to Apple or any other computer retail store. They always have computers connected to the Internet that you can use, just avoid the porn sites, OK?

Store your shit. If it looks won't have a stable sleeping situation for a while, and you don't want to sell all your stuff, look for a cheap storage unit. Many of them do killer deals for the first six months or so because they're betting on the fact that most people are too lazy to get their shit our after the first half a year is up.

Get a legit-looking PO box. If your housing situation is in the shitter, and you might have to sleep in your car or a shelter for a bit, look into getting a PO box that displays a street address as well as the box number. This way, potential employers won't know you're a bum.

Do laundry in your tub. This is exactly what it sounds like. Even better if you live in an old-school apartment with radiators for drying your clothes.

Cut the coffee. I read somewhere that when you buy coffee from a shop, the cost of the coffee lid costs more than the actual coffee in it. Get a cheap maker at home and brew it yourself. You'll probably even like yours better–plus, if you use a travel mug, you'll be way more eco-friendly.

Part 2
Actual Financial Coaching for Your Broke Ass

It's hard to even say the word "finances" without some kind of automatic twitch or eye roll. Society tells us that we are supposed to have money to buy what we need, have health insurance, take a vacation if we want to, and even know what a 401K is–but for most of us, that is not the reality. It sucks. Hard. But step no.1 to fixing this is figuring out what you can do to change it.

Unfortunately, figuring it out is a problem that most of us face at some point, including me. So for this section, I relied on the advice of **Betsy Crouch from Sizzle Consulting LLC** (coachsizzle.com). Betsy is an SF-based financial coach and consultant, who we'll call Coach Sizzle from now on. Not only is Coach Sizzle a ridiculously awesome name, but she has totally helped me kick my own ass when it comes to getting my finances in order, and I know she can help do the same for you.

While this section won't be nearly as entertaining as the the ones filled with childish poop jokes, following the advice here will actually save you tons of money. But just for good measure–poop! There. Do you feel better now?

Step 1: Face Your Finances

I know it's hard to take a good look at the man in the mirror and ask him to change his ways (yes, I just quoted a Michael Jackson song– deal with it), but that's the absolute first step in figuring out exactly how and where to begin when it comes to finances. Only you know how much anxiety and worry you feel about your situation, and only you can choose to bring that to an end.

So, the first advice from Coach Sizzle is (drumroll!):
Take her unsolicited advice.
Most people dislike unsolicited advice–you know, things like: "You shouldn't wear that"; "I wouldn't eat that" or "You should wax your upper lip." However, sometimes this advice can be like tough love and is helpful to hear. I want you to feel a greater sense of empowerment financially so you can do what makes you sizzle. Here goes: Face it! That's right. Face that financial thing that is plaguing you. Face that

thing that you are wondering and worrying about.

What you need to do is choose one simple challenge and take it on. Doing this will likely improve both your confidence and your attitude. Why do we avoid these challenges? There are so many reasons. One main reason is that many people align their net worth to their self worth. Do you do that? I'm gonna let you in on a secret: Everyone thinks everyone else has this money thing all figured out. You know what? It isn't true. Your financial situation is not who you are. You are young, broke and beautiful. Face it.

Step 2: Figure Out Where Your Money Is Going

Do you know the total of your monthly expenses? How about what you spend all your money on?

Before you start to think about creating a spending plan, debt payment plan, and/or savings plan, it's critical to know where your money is currently going (drugs, booze, midget porn). It's hard to look at it sometimes (not the midget porn, of course), and most people are surprised to see how much they spend in certain areas. Once people look at their spending, they typically realize that their perceptions about it are way off.

One of the services Coach Sizzle's company provides is basic bookkeeping and financial coaching. They create a profit and loss report and a personal expense report for their clients, who are typically independent contractors. The clients use the report as their tax preparation for their itemized expenses. Coach Sizzle says that new clients are always shocked at how much they spend on some personal expense category on the report. Sometimes people are paying for things they didn't realize they were paying for, an old bill or something they thought they cancelled. It's usually something under $15, so it slips under the radar.

Most of you probably can't afford to pay someone to track your expenses and coach you financially (*cough*–but you can submit a question to Coach Sizzle directly or check out her resources at coachsizzle.com–*cough*). If you cannot afford individual or group service, or an expensive software system, here are some free things you can do to track your expenses and to become aware of your spending:

Write down everything you spend money on for two weeks.

This recommendation comes from a fantastic book about taking the reigns of your financial life, called *Your Money or Your Life*, by Vicky Robin and Joe Dominguez. The site associated with the book is www. yourmoneyoryourlife.org. Check it out. You'll quickly see where your money is going. Most people create some shifts in habits after doing this exercise. That $5 a day for delicious mini-cupcakes really adds up, huh? Maybe you could make it them home, or buy them bulk? Mmm...cupcakes.

Use Mint.com.

Mint.com is a FREE web-based personal finance software tool. It's a great introduction to tracking your personal expenses. You set up an account, then enter all the online banking information for your credit cards and bank accounts. The site pulls your latest transactions and starts to put together a picture of your spending. You can select a category for each expense and click a box that lets the system know that every time you write a check to "Motherfucking Landlord," that it's for your personal rent, etc. Then you check in regularly to see how much you are spending for what. Is it safe? Yup, safe and secure. There's safety info on the site if you don't believe me.

Other reasons mint.com is awesome: easy budgeting, sweet graphs, suggestions on how to save money (through paid advertising from companies who want to vie for your business, but this section is not overbearing), mobile access, an iPhone app, and last but not least, you can set up text alerts to alert you if your checking account balance is low or if you went over your budget for porn last month.

Finally, you can compare your spending in a specific category, like dining, to the average person in your city and other cities. You may find that you are being really smart and frugal compared to your neighbors. If so, give yourself a pat on the back. If you find you are spending a shit-ton more than others in your city, you need to read this book over and over until you learn how to increase the awesomeness factor in your life and lowering the expense for it.

Step 3: Get Your Priorities Straight

When you spend your money, you are making a statement about your priorities. Your priorities are completely unique to you, and yours will be different from your parents', roommate's, or your friend who buys $200 shoes but says they don't have enough money to go out to eat, or the one who is buying all their groceries from the dollar store so they can save for a ski trip. It's not that they're "wasting" their money on shoes or a ski trip—maybe those things are higher priorities for them than they are for you. That's why figuring out what you should spend your hard-earned cash money on can only come from you. To figure out your financial priorities do the following:

Make a list. Write down everything you spend money on and save money for that is not a bare necessity. Do not include rent, groceries, health care needs, etc. Do include in the list "retirement" or "save for later." Also, include anything that you would like to spend money on, give money to, or save money for that you are not currently.

Rank your priorities. Start at the top of the list and compare the first item to the second item, and ask yourself, "If I could only experience 1 or 2 ,which would I choose?" Put a hash mark next to the item that "wins." Be honest. If you would rather buy clothing than give to charity, then put the hash mark next to clothing. The purpose of the exercise is to identify *your true priorities*. Repeat with 1 versus 3, 1 versus 4, and so on all the way down the list so that the first item has competed against everything. Go on to number 2 and do the same thing. When each item has "competed" against every other item, total the hash marks for each item. Write the list again, in order from the category with the highest number of hash marks to the lowest number of hash marks. These, my broke-ass friend, are your financial priorities.

Coach Sizzle says that almost every client she has ever coached has found that something about their spending and savings does not match up with their priorities. How did this turn out for you? What immediate changes can you make to align your spending and savings with your priorities?

Step 4: Save Money

Some of you may say, "I don't make enough money to save anything." If you are spending more than you are making (credit card debt) or you are making only enough to cover your basic needs, I certainly understand that you don't have money to save. For people who aren't in that position, the main thing that impacts your ability to save is how high of a priority it is. Now that you know your priorities, you are ready to make a "savings action plan," sometimes (more crudely) called "a budget."

Most people cringe at the thought of having a budget, because it sounds like you won't be able to do what you want or have any fun. But when you know your priorities, you will actually have *more* fun, because you'll be spending your money on things you want to do. Recently a client of Coach Sizzle's realized that she was spending $500-$1000 on going out each month. Now that she has identified her priorities, she is spends $100 going out and puts $400-$900 toward things that are important to her. She is still having fun, and she is a lot more excited about her finances. So, how do you make a savings action plan? So glad you asked.

Start small. It is better to save $5 a week than to save aggressively only to run into unexpected living expenses and have to withdraw the money. As you make more money or find areas to cut back, you can gradually increase the amount.

Be specific. After you've figured out your priorities from the exercise in the last section you should have a clear idea of what you are saving for. Name your savings account after whatever your savings priority is. For example, if you are passionate about traveling and create a savings account called "Travel" (or, even better: "African Safari"), you will likely be more motivated to put money into that account. Set up multiple savings accounts if need be. Ingdirect.com makes this really easy. Examples of my savings accounts are "travel," "gifts," and "fun." For research about the savings accounts with the best interest rates, I recommend searching bankrate.com.

Make it automatic. Set up savings accounts through ingdirect.com, link them to your checking account and schedule regular electronic transfers. The money is taken out of your account automatically so you don't have to worry about transferring it–or accidentally spending it on something else. Genius, right?

Could You Be Making More Money While Working Less?

While we're discussing our spending and saving habits, why not bring up the jobs that help us (or hurt us) in doing both of those things? Maybe you hate your job, or don't make enough money, but you don't feel like you can quit. Or maybe you are OK with your job but just crave some personal time to finger paint while listening to Frank Zappa in your basement. Either way, it's not crazy to want enough extra money to buy your friend a birthday drink *and* get off work in time to celebrate it.

Some advice direct from Coach Sizzle

Read the book. If your job makes you unhappy, check out *What Color Is Your Parachute?* by Richard Bolles. This great book to help you find a better fitting and higher paying job, and it's one of the best resources I've ever come across. I usually bring it up so much that people get sick of hearing about it, so just do yourself a favor and buy it or borrow it from the library.

Consider becoming a free agent. I don't work full-time, and to sustain that, I have simplified my expenses. I make less, but I have time to spend on the things I am passionate about: family, friends, and service. Could you become a freelance soloist, temp, contractor, entrepreneur, or salesperson? Are you open to creating your ideal income and work experience and *not* have to work for someone else? If so, *Free Agent Nation*, by Daniel Pink, is a fantastic resource.

Do some research. Some jobs, including things that don't mean more student loans, like bus driver and telephone operator, simply don't require as many hours per week as other jobs but pay roughly the same or better. Look into the average number of hours per week required for jobs you might be qualified for. You can also get really geeky and check out the US Dept. of Labor's *Occupational Outlook Handbook* for all kinds of info on job markets and industry outlooks.

Thanks for those tips, Coach Sizzle. You make our whisky-soaked dreams seem possible.

Step 5: Spend Your Extra Money Wisely

Extra money?! Woo-hoo! Yeah! I know that some of you reading this are thinking, *Damn, extra money? If I had some of that I could finally get that awesome tattoo I want of He-Man kicking Skeletor's ass while simultaneously giving a high-five to a Thundercat.* You know who you are.

First of all, you probably are wondering, What is "extra" money? Is it the $10 you find in your bra the morning after a hard night of partying, or is it money beyond what you needed to cover your regular monthly expenses? What about the money you have beyond covering monthly expenses and savings and retirement investments? "Extra" means something different to everyone, because each person has a different financial comfort level. One key to getting out of the cycle of "just getting by" (*ahem*, being a broke-ass) is knowing what amount you need to make to not only cover monthly expenses, but also put some loot into savings, have health insurance, and even save some money for the future. Think about the amount you are comfortable with, including living expenses and savings. Anything beyond that is "extra."

Don't do anything. So many of us think we have to "do" something with our money: We have to *buy stuff.* When you're used to barely scraping by, you think all money you have has to be spent. Wanna know how to create a little bit of financial stability when you do have some extra scratch? Just let it sit there. Don't do anything with it for a few months. Then see what happens.

Then do something. You may not be in a position of affecting your income in the short-term. We obviously can't directly affect outside forces that influence our financial opportunities. But what we can do is influence the way we think about these things and practice expanding our comfort zone. That way we're ready to seize opportunities when those fuckers present themselves.
Smart "Extra" Money Ideas

What you do with your money is a highly personal decision. But here are some suggestions.

1. Insurance: Get health insurance and renters' insurance. Health insurance for obvious reasons, and rental insurance because it protects all your personal property. If your iPod gets stolen from a bar, your renters' insurance will probably cover it. (Obviously, this differs by each policy so you check into different policies before you buy one.)

2. Cash Reserve: Most personal finance experts recommend that you have several months' worth of personal expenses in a savings account in case of unexpected situations, such as illness or losing your job. Be aware of what your bank charges for your savings account vs. the interest you receive.For example, if the monthly fee is $12 and the account pays .10 percent interest, on $5,000, you're paying $144 a year and only making $5. Not awesome. Look into online banks, because they have lower overhead expenses and therefore sometimes offer higher interest rates.

3. Savings: Where you put your money next depends on when you expect to need access to it. Think you'll need it in three to five years, or could you set it aside until you're retirement age? Planning on buying a home at some point? What about passing on your DNA to a little rugrat? Speak with a professional who focuses on giving investment advice, which I don't. Contact your local Charles Schwab office. They have great customer service and they don't try to belittle you for not having tons of moolah. Schwab.com.

Have a Spending Revolution!

"What makes life interesting is not the things you own, but the shit that you do." – Me.

That's not something I say just to make you feel better about not being able to afford Beatles Rock Band no matter how much you kill it on "I am the Walrus." It's true. Just as Coach Sizzle said, "your financial situation is not who you are." Well, neither is the amount of stuff you have.

When you spend money on anything–groceries, copy paper, or luxuries like pants without holes in them–pay attention to *where* you are doing it. Use your money, even if it's only a little bit, to make a difference by carefully choosing the companies and organizations you support.

Coach Sizzle suggests making a list of the last 15 businesses you patronized. Then ask yourself who these companies support. Do you know? Do you care? Do these companies support you? You're smart—would you buy something from someone who was rude or mean to you, or hurtful to someone or something you care about? This isn't a push to buy stuff you don't need to stimulate the economy. This is about intentionally spending your money to organizations or companies you feel are contributing positively to your community. An example of this is Carrotmob (carrotmob.org), a network of consumers who reward businesses that make the most socially responsible decisions with their patronage. You can also Google businesses that support causes you believe in, or look for telltale window stickers or decorations, such as a rainbow flag to show that a shop is LGBT-friendly.

Part 3: Financial Shit You Should Know

Overdrafts and Other Bank Bullshit

There is nothing to make you feel like an adult more than realizing you have to start asking yourself banking questions. Guess what? It's time to grow up, pal. Here are some tips on getting organized, protecting your money, and paying your bills. It is a lot sexier than it may seem.

Balance your checkbook. This means, *know the true balance of your checking account.* Seriously. You need to know your "true available balance," on a daily basis. Just because you checked your account online and see that you have $500, you don't necessarily have $500 you can spend. There may be outstanding checks that have not cleared yet, or a monthly fee that is about to be charged. Keep track of all checks you write, as well as any debit card purchases and make sure they are accounted for in your available balance. If they aren't, subtract them. I don't care how you do it. If you want to be like your Great Aunt Irma and fill in the balance of your checkbook after every single thing you spend money on, fine. The point is that knowing your true available balance will give you peace of mind. You don't have to wonder and worry whether you do or do not have the money for something. You may have to have some difficult conversations: "I can't afford that," "I can't go," or "I am going to need to pay half of my rent on the first and half on the 15th. Are you open to that?"

Many people play the "timing game," as in "I'll write this check and hope that ol' deposit goes through before my pot dealer cashes the check," or "I'll use the cash I have in there even though I wrote a check already. I hope they don't cash it!" Banks are *counting on you* to do this. They make a shitload of cash through overdrafts. Don't let them. According to Coach Sizzle, this is the cornerstone to firming up your financial foundation.

Opt out of courtesy overdraft protection. Many people rely on the overdraft protection provided by their bank as the backup system, instead of making the effort to get organized and take control of their finances. This is a crazy-expensive mistake. Most banks automatically give you overdraft protection, with fees upwards of $30 when you overdraw. That's like the mob charging you for protection—I'm pretty sure it's called racketeering, unless you're a bank. In most cases, wouldn't you prefer for your card to be declined, rather than automatically being charged a $35 fee on top of a $2 coffee purchase? A $37 cup of coffee better have been smuggled into the country in a drug mule's ass—or at least have some brandy in it. Make sure you always know your true balance, opt out of courtesy overdraft, and sign up for one of these less-expensive options.

> **1. Overdraft line of credit:** This is most preferable. If you overdraw, you're simply charged a reasonable interest rate on that amount with no ludicrously expensive fees.

> **2. Link your savings and checking accounts.** If you overdraw, the bank will dip into the savings to cover the charge. This can be problematic because many banks pay very little interest on savings accounts and if you overdraw the savings account, you'll get charged the ridiculous overdraft fees.

Link your checking account to a credit card. There is usually still an overdraft fee, around $10, and a generally poopy interest rate, which you'll need to consider if you carry a balance. Do not use a credit card that is close to its limit, as you'll be charged twice if you overdraw and go over your credit limit.

Don't sign up for automatic bill pay. One of the main causes of overdrafts is allowing companies to automatically charge your account to pay for monthly bills. What you are doing is giving the company access to your money on their terms. Let's say you are have a monthly subscription to kink.com for whatever deviant porn you're into, and you set it up to be automatically paid from your checking account. It's like saying, "Hey, Mr. Kink, whenever you feel like I owe you money, just go directly into my account and take whatever the fuck you think I owe you." Not smart. You're just fucking yourself, and not in a good way.

Coach Sizzle has a client who canceled a few business phone lines, and the phone company took $1,000 out of his checking account because he had giving them access to charge his debit card. It caused his account to be overdrawn, resulting in four overdraft charges. Once the amount has already been taken, it can be challenging to get it back. If you don't give companies access to your account, then you can challenge any bills you don't agree with beforehand. Try one of the following options instead of automatic bill pay.

1. Set up online bill pay through your checking account. If you set up automatic payments from your checking account to pay bills, enter them in your checkbook and keep them in mind when you balance your checkbook.

2. Protect your credit score. If you set up an automatic payment from your checking account to pay your credit card, make sure to set it for an amount a few dollars more than the minimum.

3. Set a limit. If you must give out your debit card information for automatic charges, authorize only a set total per month, and only do so with companies who you trust.

Your money is hard earned, or at least cleverly stolen. Don't let it be taken from you. Be powerful and protect it.

Credit Cards, Credit Scores and Other Works of Satan
To Credit Card Or Not To Credit Card...

Many folks wonder if getting a credit card will help them out of their shitty financial situation or just send them further into the crapper. The truth is, it could go either way. Here are some answers to common questions.

Should you get a credit card to get points or miles? It depends on how disciplined you are. Many people spend more using credit cards than they would using a debit card, so they end up actually paying for those points or miles with unnecessary purchases. If you're not sure whether you are disciplined enough or not, don't do it. Avoid the headaches. Set up an automatic savings plan as outlined earlier and just save up for the things you want. You'll probably have more in your pocket in the long run.

However, if you are able to set monthly spending limits and stick to them, and you pay off your credit card every month, consider getting a card that gives you points or miles but does not charge an annual fee. Coach Sizzle does not recommend American Express. To find the right card for you, check out cardtrak.com and bankrate.com.

When it comes time to cash in your points, do the math. Coach Sizzle told me that you can sometimes get more money out of your points by exchanging them for cash instead of gift cards. For example, one bank's points program charges more points for a $50 Chili's gift card than for a $50 *cash* card. Wow, they must really think their customers are dumb. Just get cash and take it to Chili's, dude.

Some cards, like Discover, give 1percent cash back on all of your purchases and 5percent on select things (for instance, grocery stores in March or retail stores in December). They'll even give 10 percent cash back if you order from their affiliated retailers (Macy's, Barnes and Noble, and a shitload more). It makes spending $100 on contacts slightly less annoying when you get $10 of it back.

Will a credit card improve your credit score? Coach Sizzle recommends getting a clear understanding of how credit scores are calculated before you make a decision to get a credit card to improve your score. Here we go.

How Credit Scores Work and Why You Should Give a Fuck
Some of you are like, "Why the fuck should I care about my credit score when I live in an expensive-ass city? It's not like I'll ever be able to afford to buy a house—and I bought my piece-of-shit car with cash." Ask yourself this: *Do you want to pay more money than other people do for the same things?* Umm...fuck no! And that's why you should care. By not paying attention to you're credit score, you're saying: "I'm totally happy to pay more for my house/car/private

student loan/other loan/etc.. I love that bank, and I want to make its executives more money so they can spend it on exotic call girls. I don't need the extra money anyway?" Yeah, really, that's exactly how you sound.

If you have been in a totally fucked financial situation and your credit is damaged as a result, I get it. I'm not criticizing you or blaming you for your situation. What I'm saying is, there are a lot of people–at all income levels–who are too laid back when it comes to credit reports and scores.

Are you listening now? Good. This is why you should care.

Reason 1: You want to keep your money.

People with better credit pay less in interest when they take out a loan. It's as simple as that.

Reason 2: You want a job.

Employers will sometimes check your credit report and score during the interview process to assess your level of responsibility. So, making late payments or defaulting on financial obligations could hinder your chances of getting hired. As much as this may seem like a breach of privacy, right now it's legal for employers to check your credit. Wack, right? Check out privacyrights.org for more about your rights regarding background checks and your credit report.

Reason 3: You want a loan—or might someday.

Government-backed student loans don't require a review of your credit history, but private lenders supposedly take on more risk lending you money because they won't be bailed out by the government. (OK, they *might* be bailed out by the government, but they'll still need to review your credit history in order to approve you for a loan.) If you have shitty credit and still manage to get approved for the loan, you'll pay more than someone with good credit (see reason 1).

Reason 4: You want a credit card.

Credit score basics was mentioned in the bit about whether to get a new credit card or not. Go back and read it. You need to understand this shit.

Reason 5: You want to move to Iowa.

It could happen. If it does, you will need to buy a car for sure, and you might even buy a house. A good credit score versus a poor credit score could save you tens of thousands of dollars in interest.

Do you care about your credit score now? Thought so. Say it with me: "I heart you, credit score!"

Now you need to show your credit score how much you love it and how sorry you are that you've been a neglectful bastard for so long.

Here's how:

1. Understand how your score is calculated. Here's the breakdown in percentages:

35%: How you pay your bills
30%: Amount of money you owe and your available credit
15%: Length of credit history
10%: Mix of credit (10%)
10%: New credit applications (10%)

2. Get copies of your reports. You can get a free copy of your credit report from each of the three credit bureaus–Experian, Equifax, and Transunion–through annualcreditreport.com. Go get on that .Ultimately, though, you'll need to purchase a report with a score. I recommend doing this through HYPERLINK "http://www.myfico. com" myfico.com. Look for discount codes online before purchasing.

3. Correct mistakes. Almost all credit reports have errors in them, so look over each report carefully. The Federal Trade Commission site has a lot of information on how to build better credit, fix errors on your report, etc. Go to ftc.gov, click on "Consumer Information," then "Credit & Loans." And you won't have to listen to that annoying freecreditreport.com band.

4. Pay on time. Thirty-five percent of your score is based on how you pay your bills, so start there. Commit yourself to paying on time every time. Linking your credit card to your checking account is a good strategy, so is setting up reminder alarms for paying bills.

Some penis-wrinkle realtor guy would not an apartment in a shitty part of San Francisco to my friend, even though his credit score was 777, because of one late payment six years earlier. What a fucking douche! "Why did you pay that late?" he asked. Seriously? Fuck you, assclown! OK, sorry. This isn't typical, and it's not meant to scare you. I just wanted to tell you a funny story about how important it is to pay bills on time.

Get professional help. Telling you how to manage your debt is like trying to summarize all the possible scenarios in a *Choose Your Own Adventure* book. Let's get real: It isn't in a credit card company's best interest for you to be educated and empowered. It is not an accident that dealing with credit and debt is confusing. The National Foundation for Credit Counseling (nfcc.org) is a Network of credit counselors. You can find one that will charge a low fee to help you manage your debt, and some will negotiate with your credit card companies. Before calling any company in the network, read about them on the Better Business Bureau's site (bbb.org).

Last But Not Least: Taxes (Shudder)

Believe it or not, my finances are pretty screwy. Shocking, right? I mean, I've gonelong periods without income and then there's my strange travel expenditures (can "experiencing" Amsterdam's Red Light District be considered a tax write-off?). Luckily I found **Keeping Your Balance**—a San Francisco-based bookkeeping, payroll, and tax preparation company—a long time ago, and they've been making sure that I get the biggest tax refund legally possible ever since, thus allowing me to continue this odd lifestyle I've become accustomed to.
    Here are a few good tax tips from Becky Shahvar of Keeping Your Balance:

If you're self employed or an independent contractor, you are not paying taxes through an employer. In addition to income tax you will need to pay self employment tax.
If you're not having taxes deducted from your paycheck,

you're required to pay taxes quarterly. It's based on your previous year tax liability. Ask your tax preparer what you should pay.

If you have a job and are getting a large refund each year, change your withholding. Talk to your tax preparer to see what you should claim.

If you have more than one job, you could be underpaying your taxes. Talk to your tax preparer if you don't want to end up with a tax balance due at the end of the year.

Be organized and keep track of your expenses so you don't lose any deductions. Keep all your receipts for the year and organize them into a different manila envelope for each month. Always file your tax return on time even if you can't pay. If you don't file, you are subject to a non-filing penalty.You can set up a payment plan to minimize penalties.

Hopefully these wise words will keep a little extra dough in your pocket in April, which you will use for (insert item here). If you didn't instantly say "a financial priority,", "a savings account," "paying off debt," or one of the other topics we just tediously covered, then please go ahead and punch yourself in the face before reading this chapter again. And, knowing you, probably one more time after that.

CONTRIBUTORS

Jill Strominger is an Ohio native and Boston University graduate who refuses to stop saying "pop" and wearing her Red Sox gear despite being heckled for doing so since moving to Brooklyn. She's been honing her thrifty ways since doing that silly thing people talk about when they ignore reason to follow their hearts and chose a career in the fulfilling but faltering music industry. She earns her beer money as a publicist and writer, and spends her spare time cooking, biking, and trying to decide if she's ready to get a cat. Jill contributed to pretty much every chapter in this book. Find her online at JillStrominger.com

Silvi Alcivar received her MFA in Creative Nonfiction writing from The Pennsylvania State University and earned a BA in English and Women's Studies, with a focus on fine art, from the College Scholar program at Cornell University. Her work has been published in online journals and in Poets 11: a collection of poems edited by Jack Hirschman. She has performed her work, on stage and radio, throughout the San Francisco Bay area. Currently, she is the owner of a small business, The Poetry Store, in which she writes and sells custom poetry in three forms: on-demand, as jewelry, and as art. Silvi wrote the amazing poem that starts this book off. Fine her online at ThePoetryStore.net [photo by Julie Michelle]

Betsy Crouch, "Coach Sizzle," is a coach, speaker, and writer, who has financially coached over 350 clients in their 20s and 30s. She'll help you to clarify your values and show you how to align your investment of time, money, and energy, with your true priorities. Why? So you can find peace with money, be yourself, sizzle, and thrive! You may be broke but you aren't *broken!* Visit www.coachsizzle.com.

Zora O'Neill has lived on the cheap in NYC since 1998, all thanks to the wonders of home cooking. She's the coauthor of Forking Fantastic: Put the Party back in Dinner Party and blogs at www.rovinggastronome.com [photo by Peter Moskos]

Sarah M. Smart was summoned into being on a distant ice cream planet through an unholy union of Two-Buck Chuck and unicorns. They sent her to Indianapolis and then the University of Missouri's School of Journalism to spread peace and big hair. Perpetually in mourning for the comma, she has worked for a variety of print media, including Indianapolis Monthly, Global Journalist, and Vox. Since moving to San Francisco for the booming dumpster-diving scene, she has been an online operative for such fine folks as Horoscope.com , Neo-Factory, and Academy of Art University. Sarah contributed the section on how to make your own home bar. You can find her at SarahMSmart.com, Vegansaurus.com and BrokeAssStuart.com.

Kate Kotler is the founding editor of Geek Girl on the Street.com and has reprised the DIY Diva column which began on Broke Ass Stuart's Goddamn Website in 2009 for ChicagoNow (part of the esteemed Chicago Tribune, fancy right?) Kate loves sushi, The Chicago Cubs, Doctor Who, her Mom, Frank Miller, Wonder Woman, knitting, decoupage, cheap travel and beer, puppetry and she used to be a professional fire-eater. She lives in Chicago with her adorable doggie, Max. Kate contributed to both the travel and beauty chapters. She can be found online at KateKotler.com [photo by Julie Michelle]

Following several fuzzy years learning how to creatively abuse punctuation in the University of Virginia's English department (no endorsement implied), **Andrew Dalton** arrived in San Francisco with the goal of joining the Internet revolution. After a few years spent raiding office supplies from local ad agencies and accepting free lunches from sales reps, he found his calling banging away at a keyboard for a variety of Bay Area publications. He can generally be found hovering over a laptop or glass of decent whiskey. Andrew contributed to the travel chapter, the financial chapter and also let you know how to get press passes for being "members of the press". Visit him online at Dolfapedia.org.

Anna G. is a Southern California native living in the Williamsburg area of Brooklyn since 2005. Anna is constantly trying to unite her love of CA sunshine and the excitement of the New York urban jungle, all the while trying to keep her unwieldy credit card debt under control, and look fabulous at brunch, no matter how un-showered and hungover. Anna contributed advice on how to deal with long distance relationships. She's been writing for the Sex and Dating section of BrokeAssStuart.com since its inception.

Like most kids, **Ashley Friedman** grew up in New Jersey. Unlike most kids the Friedman's televison set acted as a third parent, imbuing young Ashley with the stern moral values of Claire Huxtable, the dramatic tendencies of Brenda Walsh and the earnest hopefulness of the blond kid on Silver Spoons. After graduating from Sarah Lawrence College, Ashley made her way to to Brooklyn where she enjoys eating in restaurants, scouring stores for vintage heels, streaming 90s sit-coms on her laptop and stretching her meager income as far as it will go in NYC. Ashley contributed the section called "The Upside of Being Unemployed". Find her online at MyPainIsSoSignificant.tumblr.com

Since leaving the "sixth borough" to see what this New York thing was all about, **Laura Smith** has been chronicling her adventures of fame and misplaced fortune to anyone who will listen. While doling out meaningful and yet often misguided advice, she's willing to trying anything in the name of gaining life experience even if that means eating every sandwich in the city named the Godfather. She believes the best experiences in life cannot be bought but only lived. Laura lives in Brooklyn. She is the NYC editor for BrokeAssStuart.com

Stephen Torres spent his early years in a boxcar overlooking downtown Los Angeles before moving up and down the central Californian coast. He lives mostly in San Francisco, although he's packed his belongings in a kerchief from time to time to wander around here and there. In addition to BrokeAssStuart.com, he has also written for the San Francisco Bay Guardian and The Bold Italic. Stephen contributed to the travel chapter of this fine book.

A writer and editor based out of San Francisco, **Amber Bouman** currently works for MaximumPC.com and writes a DIY column for Broke-Ass Stuart. She has written for PCWorld, InfoWorld, SFWeekly and Spinning Platters; her poetry has appeared in the 16th & Mission Review and the Altered Barbie commemorative book and she has performed at dozens of venues. She can be found in various virtual locations all over your interwebs, including amberbouman.com. Amber contributed the knowledge of how to infuse your own vodka.

Kiley Edgley is a writer who has published work on everything from the Kentucky Derby to insect reproduction. She regularly alters her clothes on the night she plans to wear them out, and is more likely to be carrying electrical tape than chapstick. She reads National Geographic for the articles. Currently, she lives in a lovely basement in Brooklyn, NY. Kiley contributed to the section of how to Behave in a Restaurant. Find her online at kwolverine.blogspot.com

Oliver Hartman is a freelance writer, independent filmmaker, and guerilla tennis instructor living in NYC. He has worked as a waiter, tutor, cocktail boy, model, door man, bartender, fact-checker, copy writer, and web marketer. He also moves friends' furniture for meals and recently co-founded the NYC based production company GuyManly. Oliver contributed the recipe for making your own Kahlua. You can find him online at oliverhartman.com.

Originally from San Diego, **Heidi Smith** migrated north to study journalism at SFSU and interned for the *SF Bay Guardian* writing music stuff. She later embarked on a study-abroad program in both Denmark and Holland, and basically never came home. For six long years, she froze her ass off in Oslo, Norway, pretending to be a viking princess, trying to figure out how to survive in the most expensive city in the world. The other two years were spent frolicking on the beach in Spain - sipping on sangria in between being tossed around Europe working as a stressed-out journalist. Heidi currently works at for a non-profit cultural exchange program, helping others experience life from a different perspective. She is thrilled to be back in SF, magnetizing the obscure, and scavenging the city for fun, free things to do. Heidi contributed to the Making Money section. You can find her online at Cultureshock-HSmith.blogspot.com

Mike Force is an illustrator and designer living in Seattle after spending a decade in Brooklyn. He created the Poster Museum pop-up shop featuring top Seattle designers including Art Chantry, Shawn Wolfe and Jeff Kleinsmith. He has contributed to *Vice*, *The L Magazine*, *Brooklyn Magazine*, icanhascheesburger.com, *Businessweek Magazine*, *The Stranger*, *The Portland Mercury* and many others. www.autotone.net

Thanks

First and foremost I'd like to thank the good folks at Seven Footer for their patience and for putting out this book so I wouldn't have to do all this shit by myself. Thanks to Sam Erickson and the 44 pictures crew for helping me make amazing TV and for being the Wandering Invincible Circus. Thanks to IFC for giving me a chance and seeing my potential.

I'd also like to thank all the contributors who helped to make this book the essence of pure awesomeness that it is and let me use their work: Thanks to Jill Strominger for coming in and helping get this book done in time. It wouldn't have been possible without her. Thanks to Silvi Alcivar for her beautiful poem. Thanks to Betsy Crouch for her sage financial coaching. Thanks to Zora O'Neill for her awesome recipes. Thanks to Sarah M. Smart for her home bar tips. Thanks to Kate Kotler for her beauty and travel advice. Thanks to Andrew Dalton for his travel, financial and entertainment advice, as well as for his tenure as SF editor of BrokeAssStuart.com. Thanks to Anna G. for her always hilarious sex and dating advice as well as for being a good friend for the past 10 years. Thanks to Ashley Friedman for her tips on how to enjoy being unemployed as well as her kick-ass reign as the NYC editor of BrokeAssStuart.com. Thanks to Laura Smith for her tips on using babysitting as exercise and for doing a great job as the current NYC editor on BrokeAssStuart.com. Thanks to Stephen Torres for his tips on travel and for being part of the SF team almost since its inception. Thanks to Amber Bouman for her vodka infusing capabilities and her fantastic DIY column. Thanks to Kiley Edgly for sharing in the restaurant server struggle and for being a part of the NYC team for so long. Thanks to Oliver Hartman for his Kahlua recipe, his time as the first NYC editor, and for his numerous years as a good friend. Thanks to Heidi Smith for her ideas on making money. Thanks to Mike Force for all the design work throughout the past three books. Thanks to Sam Erickson, Julie Michelle, and Victoria Smith for being so kind as to take photos of me and let me use them.

Thanks to Krista, my amazing and beautiful girlfriend, for being my partner, for loving me, and for putting up with all my bullshit. I know I'm not the easiest person to date, but I love you. Thanks to my parents for being supportive and not being disappointed that I didn't want to grow up to be a doctor, lawyer or an accountant. Thanks to my brother Ross for being just being Ross. Thanks to my Grandma Blanche for thinking I'm cool no matter what my current endeavors are. Thanks to all my aunts, uncles and cousins for helping me spread my message. Thanks to my Grandpa Bob and my Grandma Ethel who both passed away in the last year, but who were always supportive of this weird life that I've chosen. I miss you both. Thanks to all the friends who have believed in me throughout the years and have supported by buying books and merch, and showing up to all the weird events I throw. My success is 100% because of the love and support that all of the people in this past paragraph have shown me.

Thanks to all the wonderful people who gave me their own personal tips, advice and knowledge on how to survive life as a broke-ass: Gabi Moskowitz, Becky Shahvar, Alex Maiolo, Ethan Wolff, Ken Scarince, Geoff King, Ed DeHahn, Amie Vaccaro, Natalie Galatzer, Ebony Koger, Kevin Montgomery, Lili Toutounas, , David Peisner, Nick Perotta, and anyone else I may have accidentally forgotten (I'm kind of a dumbass sometimes).

Also, thanks to all anyone who has ever written for BrokeAssStuart.com but whose stuff didn't get included in this book: Monica Miller, Christy Jovanelly, Joe Peterson, Chloe Roth, Alison Lambert, Rebecca Pederson, Danielle Levanas, Christine Witmer, Polina Yamshchikov,

Mikey Rox, Ricardo Bilton, Katy B, Jessica Longo, Dan Cerruti, Mia Di Pasquale, Chris Fielder, Bobby Rich, Patrick Poelvoorde, Steven K, Rebecca E. Once again, sorry if I forgot anyone!

Thanks to Michael Curran for being my web guru. Thanks to Kenny Liu for being my original partner in all things broke-ass. Thanks to Michael Silver and Ric Cohen for being the absolutely best attorneys ever! Thanks to Man Down for helping me navigate the weird ass entertainment industry.

Thanks to the City and County of San Francisco for loving me nearly as much as I love it. Thanks to New York City for keeping me bi-coastal curious. Thanks to Anthony Bourdain for giving me something to strive towards. Thanks to Tapatio salsa for making everything taste better.

Thanks to all of you who've bought this book and are on the front lines of the Broke-Ass Revolution. I wrote it for you. And most of all I would like to thank anyone who ever bought any of the zines, books, shirts or other merch I've done in the past. Your support mean the world to me.

I love all of you! Thank you (just thought I'd throw one more in there for good luck).